Loneliness and Spiritual Growth

Loneliness and Spiritual Growth

SAMUEL M. NATALE

Religious Education Press
Birmingham, Alabama

Library of Congress Cataloging-in-Publication Data

Natale, Samuel M.
  Loneliness and spiritual growth.

  Includes bibliographies and index.
  1. Loneliness.   2. Loneliness—Religious aspects.
3. Developmental psychology.   I. Title.
BF575.L7N37   1986   155.9′2   86-10012
ISBN 0-89135-055-1

Religious Education Press, Inc.
1531 Wellington Road
Birmingham, Alabama 35209
10 9 8 7 6 5 4 3 2

Religious Education Press publishes books exclusively in religious education and in areas closely related to religious education. It is committed to enhancing and professionalizing religious
education through the publication of serious, significant, and
scholarly works.

PUBLISHER TO THE PROFESSION

For

GERALD C. HAMM, PH.D.
—MENTOR AND FRIEND

And when he had sent the multitude away,
he went up into the mountain apart to pray:
and when the evening was come, he was
there alone.

Matthew 14:23

Contents

Preface

Loneliness is epidemic in our culture. From the distraught cries of the infant separated from its caretaker to the haunting image of an aging adult who is cut off by illness or death from loved ones, the images proliferate in our world. The growing body of empirical research suggests that loneliness is more than an unpleasant feeling—it is a killer!

Anyone can be lonely independent of the number of friends, family, or social contacts which one has. It has been suggested that as many as 25 percent of the population experiences acute loneliness. The popular texts that deal with handling loneliness continue to be "best sellers." Anyone working directly with people from all walks of life has had the opportunity to observe that many are lonely and isolated. Traditionally, these problems have been assuaged, at least by those who were able to sustain involvement, by membership in extended family groups, church organizations, and other communally based experiences. These "remedies" are clearly not able to accommodate in the way they used to as we find more and more people cut off from their nuclear family because of emotional conflict or career development. The churches seem to be unable to respond as well. The traditional focus on either the scripture or on the more liberally based counseling model has become

1

increasingly—and obviously—less effective.

Loneliness is a state which involves a *conscious* lack of friendship, warmth, and contact. This is often exacerbated by feelings of being "no good" or "unlovable" and manifests itself by difficulties in forming *satisfactory* relationships with other people. As we explore the manifestations of loneliness throughout the life cycle and designate the definitive intervention which appropriate religious/ethical education can have, it will be important to keep ourselves aware that in our definition there are two controlling concepts: *conscious* and *satisfactory*. We will discuss these ideas later, but it is crucial to state at the outset that the feelings and experiences we are speaking about when we discuss loneliness are *not* identical to solitude or aloneness. Loneliness in our definition involves a "conscious" lack which means that the person experiences being without others in a clear and negative way. Further, the person must have as a remedy "satisfactory" relationships. That is to say, if a person is surrounded by people but does not find them nurturing or enlivening, then they may well be experiencing an acute loneliness even though to the casual observer these people have many friends and family/community members.

There is hope! As we explore the life cycle and the insights which religious education and social science offer, we shall begin to see that there are not only ways *out* of the morass but avenues of positive growth and challenge.

Many of the remedies for loneliness arise from recent developments in religious education and social science. I am speaking here of a rigorous education in religion which calls upon the state-of-the-art insights and techniques in philosophy and social science. This has been most adequately developed by James Michael Lee at the University of Alabama at Birmingham and John Wilson, Fellow of

Mansfield College in the University of Oxford, England. A rigorous and analytical approach to religious education, doing no damage to revelation, forces individuals to reexamine their values, attitudes, needs, and expectations in light of their personal development and in tune with current empirical thought.

Throughout this book, the emphasis on empirical thought and research will be constant. My position is that if something "works" then it is important to see that this is reflected in actual behaviors of individuals. It is useless to speak of a religious or ethical education which remedies problems and then to explain it to an eager audience in terms so woolly that nothing can be verified. Over and over again we will attempt to integrate theory and practice and explore possible interpretations of the empirical studies we have analyzed or directly undertaken.

I am particularly grateful to Darlene Pienta as well as Darby Kishibay for their active research assistance. I am also indebted to Richard Grande for his technical assistance in the writing and preparation of this manuscript. Most importantly, I am grateful to the intellectual leadership provided to me by John Wilson of the University of Oxford and the keen and critical eye of James Michael Lee of Religious Education Press for seeing the value in this project and encouraging me on toward completion.

A Mellon Fellowship from the University of Bridgeport, Connecticut, and a Visiting Scholarship to St. Edmund House in the University of Cambridge gave me the scholarly resources to complete this study.

A word of special praise is due to Caroline Mathuse who with very limited time and undue pressure was able to complete this manuscript in a professional and cheerful way.

Chapter 1

Loneliness and the Problem of Definition

Who has not heard the challenge, "It's easier said than done?" It is understood in this example that verbalizing solutions is only a first and perhaps easier step than enacting them. There are situations, however, in which the challenge can be reversed. In this case the sentence might read, "It's hard to say what actually happened." That is, there are so many different ways of considering what happened, that any single interpretation might not be sufficient or accurate. Naming the experience is often more difficult than starting with the "name" and attempting to "do" what is named. A nationally syndicated cartoon is called "Love is . . ." and every day, 365 days a year, a different picture accompanies the caption, "Love is . . ." We all have our own idea of what love is, but our actual experiences of love are so alike and yet so different that a single definition seems too miserly for this global experience.

The experience of loneliness is also difficult to definè. Some might ask, "Why define an experience that most people have felt? Why not just let it be and draw from it." I assume that analyzing so universal a concept as loneliness may result in critical understandings for human growth that may not be available if we were to "just let it be and draw from it" (Peplau, Russell, & Heim, 1979).

5

It is sometimes the very commonplace that is overlooked in the search for the sophisticated solution. Cancer researchers are aware that the cure for this disease may lie in the most common and usual of our lives. There are medical speculations that point to some association between histories of personal loss and the onset of cancer (Hartog, 1980). Physical disease hardly seems transferable to our loved ones. But is that what is transferred?

If a theory of loneliness helps persons to understand and so name their experience, it seems well worth the effort to construct such a theory. Naming the phenomenon is only a portion of the solution, but it is a substantial portion. For loneliness is a common experience. Yet the uncommon events of suicides, broken hearts, and psychoses have been linked to loneliness (Lynch, 1976). The question for the inquirer is why, if so many persons experience loneliness, are there not more suicides, more broken hearts, more psychoses? Why do some escape these extremes and not others (Weiss, 1982)? We might pose the same question with cancer. Do the answers reside within or outside of the person, or both (Perlman & Peplau, 1982)? Answers that may emerge seem to do so largely as a result of the direction of the questioning. This book will pursue a specific direction that may reveal where the questions lie, rather than the answers. A first task will be to review the research that has investigated the phenomenon of loneliness. A second task will be to draw implications for religious and ethical educators stemming from this research. My theory of loneliness will be within this section. This two-part approach follows a process of observe, judge, and act. Its problem-solving method is based on the assumption that loneliness is a problem in that it signifies deficit (Flanders, 1982). Many persons express an emptiness, a "hole" in their lives when trying to articulate loneliness. How do we, who experience loneliness, deal with it? How do we, who face the lonely in our classrooms, within our acquaintances, within ourselves help move beyond this deficit?

I. What Is Loneliness?

In order to define an experience such as loneliness, it is usually important to talk about it, to analyze experiences of it, to measure it. Surprisingly, for so global a phenomenon, relatively scant attention has been given to loneliness. A number of reasons are given for this. An obvious one is that its presence seems to connote failure (Goswick & Jones, 1981). It is embarrassing for persons to admit to loneliness. A corollary thought is based on an unspoken assumption that if persons are lonely, it is their task to find a solution as if the loneliness is due to and remedied solely by their personal initiative. Continued loneliness is looked upon as perhaps "not really trying." In this case, loneliness is viewed as a person-centered affliction which the person must control by some willed effort. Admissions of loneliness are met with advice on how to eliminate the condition. Often the advice takes the form of "get out and meet people."

What one author calls "transient" loneliness is not often the center of research among psychologists, sociologists, or anthropologists. Each of these disciplines deals with more extreme forms of loneliness. The psychologist treats experiences of anomie or depression; the sociologist writes of alienation; the anthropologist compares the solitude experiences of different cultures. Is loneliness depression or alienation or anomie? Who then deals with loneliness? Any or all of the above?

Researchers are beginning to recognize the importance of studying loneliness as a unique experience. The early

seminal work of H. S. Sullivan and Frieda Fromm-Reichmann is being reviewed and considered for the insights
which it offers. Perhaps more importantly, a more holistic
perspective on the causes of loneliness is considering person and situation as dual, rather than separate "either-or"
contributors to that experience.

A number of approaches will be reviewed in this book.
Past definitions of loneliness have come primarily from
clinical work. Sociological analysis and research have added to our understanding of loneliness. Table 1 offers a
comprehensive overview of current work on loneliness.
Each approach is grounded in a particular philosophy. Before discussing the ramifications of these approaches, it is
important to notice the two, two-part distinction of ontological assumptions of nature and cause. Regarding the
nature of loneliness, the word "positive" is used to determine if loneliness is considered an asset. Only the existentialist affirms this. Also, the words "normal" or "pathological" are used with obvious meaning. Only the psychodynamic and phenomenological view considers loneliness as
pathological. The others give a more normal assessment
with the exception of the existential and sociological which
includes individual nuances of "normal" (i.e., "universal"
and "normative").

A second set of distinguishing assumptions concerns the
causes of loneliness. A person vs. an environmental perspective is considered as well as developmental vs. current
causes. Noticeable in this analysis is the unanimity of the
more recent approaches (interactionist, cognitive, etc.) in
their assessment of basic cause. I believe that the "systems"
and "cognitive" approach as outlined by their authors[1]
would disagree with the "current" designation for developmental vs. current and would most likely list "both" for
that perspective.

Table 1. Eight Approaches to Loneliness[2]

	Psycho-dynamic	Phenome-nological	Existen-tial	Socio-logical	Interac-tionist	Cognitive	Privacy	Systems
Views tied to	Clinical work	Clinical work	Clinical work	Social analysis	Clinical work	Research	Theory	Theory
Nature of loneliness								
Positive	No	No	Yes	No	No	No	No	Yes
Normal or pathological	Pathological	Pathological	Universal	Normative	Normal	Normal	Normal	Normal
Causes								
Within the person or the situation	Person	Person	Human condition	Society	Both	Both	Both	Both
Historical and childhood vs. current	Childhood	Current	Perpetual	Both	Current	Current	Current	Current

Regardless of the root assumptions driving these analyses, there are three points of agreement among the majority of scholars. First, loneliness is a result of a social deficit; second, the experience of loneliness is unpleasant; and lastly, people can be alone without being lonely or, on the other hand, be in a crowd and be lonely (Peplau & Perlman, 1982). The following discussion will review the research that substantiates these commonalities.

Loneliness and Relationship

Robert S. Weiss (1973) provided an impetus for recent research (Peplau & Perlman, 1982; Brennan & Auslander, 1979; McCallister & Fischer, 1978). As the title implies, Weiss identifies two affective states which are called loneliness. *Emotional* isolation is the absence of an accessible social network. In describing this and other research, these two concepts of emotional and social isolation will be combined into a single concept of relationship (Peplau et al., 1982). At times we will deal with relationship to the "one" (or its opposite, emotional isolation) and at other times with relationship to the "many" (or its opposite, social isolation).

Research by Fischer and Phillips (1982) found that defining and measuring isolation was as difficult as defining and measuring loneliness. They, however, chose to deal with this problem by looking at isolation from the standpoint of "how many friends (or kin)" and "how often do you see friends (or kin)"? Their findings revealed a complex pattern in isolation from kin and nonkin. Isolation from kin seemed to cause individuals to seek nonkin and isolation from nonkin had a substantial association with unhappiness. Significant results showed uneducated and poor more isolated from nonkin, with kin relationships not sufficient to affect their higher loneliness scores. Generally, they found that "access to and participation in various social contexts determines isolation" (Fischer & Phillips, 1982).

The Fischer and Phillips (1982) research found that married men are protected from kin isolation and are provided with at least one confidant and therefore tend to be less lonely. This finding was repeated in other studies (Haas-Hawkings, 1978; Tunstall, 1967). On the whole, married persons tend to be less lonely than separated, divorced, widowed, or single respondents. Widowed and single respondents are found to be less lonely than the separated and divorced (Rubenstein & Shaver, 1982).

A number of studies found that friendship is a most influential factor in loneliness. Cutrona's study (1982) of college students found that the degree of satisfaction with current friendships was a better predictor of Loneliness Scale scores than was satisfaction with either dating or family relationships. She further reported that the quality and not the quantity of relationships was critical in staving off loneliness. This view is one supported by Rook and Peplau (1982).

Russell (1982) supported several studies that found the lonely more hostile, less responsive, and less aggressive in inquiring about the other (Jones, 1982; Horowitz, French, & Anderson, 1982). In a study by Jones (1982), the issue of intimacy was treated.

Among opposite sex dyads, lonely as compared to nonlonely subjects chose less intimate topics on both their first topic choice and the average of all topic choices. Within same sex dyads, lonely subjects selected a more intimate first topic than did nonlonely subjects. Thus the behavior of lonely subjects during interpersonal interactions with opposite sex strangers may be characterized as more self focused and less responsive (p. 248).

The issues of intimacy and self-concept are directly related. Russell's results showed lonely students reflecting a greater discrepancy between self and reflected self concepts than did nonlonely students (Russell, 1982). Horowitz, French, and Anderson (1982) found lonely people less able to find solutions to written situations concerning interpersonal relations. This finding is even more significant in light of these same people performing similarly to nonlonely persons in dealing with impersonal situations.

Research dealing with adolescents show significant loneliness scores. One explanation given for this is the developing sense and need for intimacy that accompanies adolescence (Sullivan, 1953). The research of Derlega and Marqulis (1982) on "privacy" links self-disclosure and intimacy (Derlega & Grzelak, 1979). Intimacy depends on self-disclosure, that is, it depends on regulating the personal or self boundary. A common complaint is, "I find it hard to make friends in a simple, natural way" (Horowitz & French, 1979). There is an inability to relate to others in a mutually satisfying manner (Jones, 1982). This need to relate to a significant other is so strong at adolescence that frustration in attaining this goal results in an experience of loneliness that is significant enough to substantially differentiate this age group from older persons (Sadler & Johnson, 1980). An observation by Sadler and Johnson provides further insight into the turmoil of adolescence.

> We may not always be able to articulate or communicate our feelings, but we must be able to feel our feelings as emotions, we must be (self)consciously aware of experiencing an emotion (p. 67).

Considering the varied and intense emotions of adolescence, it is not difficult to understand that regardless of a verbalizing ability, sorting out loneliness for special mention may be an extremely difficult task.

Special attention was given to adolescents because of research supporting this age group as most lonely. The other part of these data shows older respondents least lonely (Lowenthal, Thurner, & Chiriboga, 1976; Dyer, 1974). One explanation for this difference is that older persons have fewer expectations regarding relationships.

Part of reacting to any expectation is being able to identify the experience at hand. As noted above, the adolescent may have a more difficult time in initially identifying loneliness.[3] The older person, while perhaps more able to identify the experience also has lowered expectations of what is possible.[4] Relationships with others tell us what is possible, what we can expect. Although research shows the quantity of relationships a secondary issue to quality, there is some merit to a multitude of experiences fashioning our sense of expectation. "Our self-conception is largely based on our relationships to other people—as friend, lover, parent, child, neighbor, co-worker" (Peplau, Miceli, & Morasch, 1982; p. 147). The adolescent, by virtue of age, has had less opportunity for multiple relationships.

Cutrona and Peplau (1982) found that students' perceptions that their relationships were worse than their peers were significantly linked to loneliness. Clinicians are aware that lonely people often evaluate themselves and others negatively. Thus the self-concept enters into evaluations and expectations. Young (1982) uses this understanding to construct a cognitive theory of loneliness. He says, "The way individuals view relationships is perhaps the most important determinant of how satisfying their friendships are and therefore of how lonely they are" (p. 379).

Cutrona (1982) advises that unrealistic standards or expectations may provide a clue to alleviating loneliness.

Once these social demands can be scaled to the situation, the individual may be well on the way to social equanimity and happiness (Lederer & Jackson, 1968). Fromm-Reichmann whose 1959 work on loneliness was one of the first dealing directly with the topic, cautions that individuals' primary sense of isolation may be reinforced if they cannot differentiate between realistic phenomenon and products of their own fantasy.

An interesting adjunct to this "expectation" thought is the reference of several researchers to "perceptions of control." One writer speaks of the degree of control that individuals maintain over their self-disclosure (Peplau, Miceli, & Morasch, 1982). Another perspective is the sense of hope for improving relationships that resides in "control" (Peplau et al, 1982). The question arises as to the influence that control or lack of it has on loneliness. If self-disclosure is a critical ingredient for intimacy and so for a relationship with a significant other, then being in control of that process takes on a more substantive role. It is established that "trying too hard" (i.e., disclosing too much or inappropriate information) can be as detrimental to friendship as too little disclosure. Significantly, research has shown the lonely to have an external locus of control, i.e., some power outside the person is controlling. Facilitating, if possible, the development of an internal locus seems a priority in those treating the lonely.

One last issue, "spiritual well-being" has been considered as a general factor in loneliness research. Paloutzian and Ellison (1982) found an inverse association between spiritual well-being and loneliness. Their inference was that loneliness is one indicator of the quality of life. Zimbardo (1979) found that for most of the 2 billion who expressed religious affiliation, life and its experiences were assessed by reference to this commitment. Using a Spiritual Well-

Being Scale (SWB), the authors were able to show that people who scored high on the SWB tended to be less lonely, more socially skilled, higher in self-esteem, and more intrinsic in their religious commitment (Paloutzian & Ellison, 1982). They measured three types of variables: social context, developmental background, and values. They supported Shaver and Rubenstein's (1980) findings that greater intimacy during childhood is associated with less loneliness during adulthood. Using the social context of marriage, they found that whether a woman was satisfied with her marriage and living situation was more important than what her situation happened to be.

Values were also found to influence interpersonal trust and a sense of belonging and community. However, several questions remained unanswered, such as how early childhood factors affect adult loneliness and the possible roles of values in determining loneliness.

The above discussion has not dealt in any depth with "traits" of the lonely. While relationship seems to be most related to the feeling of loneliness, there is some evidence that personal traits do influence relationship. Therefore, some attention will now be given to this question of personality.

Young (1982) identifies three kinds of loneliness, situational, chronic, and transient, based on the length of time an individual has been lonely. Chronic loneliness is when, over a period of years, a person is not able to develop satisfying social relations. Situational loneliness often follows some major life stress event, such as death of a spouse or ending of a marriage. Transient loneliness is the most common form and refers to shorter bouts with feeling lonely. Young relies on Beck's cognitive theory to support his loneliness therapy.

According to Beck (1976), the way individuals structure

their experiences is significantly related to how a person feels and acts. These personal meanings—view of the self and environment—form the basis for an individual's "internal reality" (p. 50). Young continues then to construct therapeutic methods based on a matching of internal and external reality. For the present, however, I am interested in using this reference to "internal reality" as it reflects and affects personality. It seems to be closely connected to the above discussion on expectation. Expectation in turn, makes a substantial contribution to the self-fulfilling prophecy.

Jones (1982) has suggested that the combination of perceiving and being perceived as lonely may be implicated in the persistence of loneliness. Furthermore, individuals who perceive their educational, occupational, and recreational opportunities as blocked score higher on the loneliness scale. Lonely persons are found to have an intense longing, without which, at least one author has suggested, persons are not truly lonely. This author describes longing as an "anxious, painful, indescribable yearning for someone or something" (Hartog, 1980). Another writer defines loneliness as a "set of sentiments and emotions accompanying dissatisfaction with one's past, present, or future levels or forms of social relations" (Lopata et al, 1982).

Young, especially, pursues this notion of a "set of sentiments and emotions." He describes what he calls "clusters" of cognition, behavior, and emotion. He explains that these clusters do not define loneliness but rather they seem to predispose the individual to feel lonely and maintain the loneliness (Young, 1982). Selected examples of the clusters are shown in Table 2.[5]

Part of this cognitive-behavioral model is directed at teaching the lonely first to recognize "automatic thoughts"

Table 2. Loneliness Clusters

Name of Cluster	Typical Automatic Thoughts	Typical Maladaptive Assumptions	Typical Behaviour	Typical Emotions
1. Low self-concept	1. I'm undesirable. 2. I'm ugly. 3. I'm dull and boring. 4. I can't change the way I am.	1. People are completely intolerant of other people's faults. 2. It's essential to be attractive, intelligent, lively, witty etc., to have any friends.	Avoidance of other people.	Sad, hopeless, worthless.
2. Problems in partner selection	1. There's no place to meet the opposite sex. 2. The men and women I get involved with always end up hurting me. 3. There are very few men/women I find desirable. 4. No one can measure up to my last lover. 5. The partners I find attractive will not be acceptable to my friends or to society.	1. I must find the perfect man/woman and not settle for less. 2. I should continue to pursue people I am strongly attracted to, regardless of whether we are well-suited in other respects. 3. If I just try hard enough, I can always get the man/woman I want to love me.	Lor rate of initiating potentially intimate relationships or pattern of selecting inappropriate partners.	Frustrated, hopeless, emotionally empty, bitter.

and, second, to look upon them as hypotheses to be tested rather than as unchangeable facts.

Certain personal characteristics are beginning to be linked with loneliness. Lonely people are apt to be shy, introverted, less willing to take social risks. They lack social skills, are generally uneducated, poor, not working, or have low incomes. Obviously this is a mixture of personal and situational factors with "and/or" between each description. Which factors contribute to the others is a question which is just beginning to be seriously addressed in defining loneliness and its causes. It is this more total picture of person *and* situation that Flanders' (1982) "General Systems" approach to loneliness attempts to address. In this theory, loneliness is conceptualized as "an adaptive feedback mechanism" for bringing the individual from a current lack of stress to a more optimal range of human contact. The theory sees the environment as influencing this feedback mechanism and therefore in need of control to afford "optimal contact" for the individual.

II. Loneliness As Unpleasant

The previous discussion has dealt with the fact of loneliness. There is an implicit notion that loneliness is unpleasant and therefore must be alleviated if not eliminated completely. There are, however, those who see loneliness in a more positive light, who while not advocating loneliness approach it as a desirable and even necessary experience. Although loneliness is being explored as a unique experience, other similar experiences continue to be linked to it. Their connection with loneliness in either leading to it or as a result of it causes some confusion as to the merit of or liability of loneliness. These experiences are depression, aloneness, and solitude.

While the four terms, loneliness, depression, aloneness, and solitude, are somewhat clustered together and at times used interchangeably, there are nuances which are important to recognize. An accurate understanding of each of these experiences can help the clinician as well as individuals who seek to do their own analysis and adjustment in effectively dealing with each or a combination of these emotions.

As noted earlier, the existentialist views loneliness as a given. It is a basic condition of life. Mijuskovic (1980) expresses this view when he says, "Now in saying this I do not mean that we think or feel we are alone all the time and at every moment; I think we really are, but we are not always aware of it" (p. 68). Loneliness, then, serves as a precondition for companionship. By itself it is valueless; it has no positive or negative value until it is confronted by its opposite—an opportunity for community.

A similar view is given by Flanders (1982) who in his "general systems" approach to loneliness, says that loneliness should not be eliminated. Rather it should be controlled because it is a "valuable feedback mechanism with important survival value to both the individual and the nation" (p. 178). Moustakas supports this in his widely read work, *Loneliness* (1961). Sadler and Johnson (1980) agree with this basic positive stance regarding loneliness, but they draw back from the strict existentialist view that individuals are "utterly and forever alone." They qualify their position by positing individuals' personal world as complex, and so while loneliness is an important "signal" from the network it is neither the most important nor the most authentic one.

Sadler and Johnson speak of multiple dimensions of loneliness. When people are affected by only one dimension of loneliness they seem well able to cope with the distress. When, however, they face loneliness on more than one dimension, the ensuing stress, where it comes from and how to "divide and conquer," is sometimes difficult to manage.

Young's clusters might be thought of as dimensions in Sadler's and Johnson's sense of the word. This intense stress may lead to anomie. "It is our contention that anomie, at least in many instances, is a consequence of severe unresolved loneliness encountered on two or more dimensions within a person's world" (p. 58).

It seems that depression, a negative manifestation of loneliness, might be found within this context of more than one dimension of loneliness. Other writers, however, contend that depression and loneliness are not coextensive. That is, those who are depressed *may* also be lonely and those who are lonely *may* become depressed (Horowitz, French, & Anderson, 1982; Bragg, 1979). In other words, although they share common causal origins, they have quite different potential. Several authors have also supported the cognitive view that whether persons respond to loneliness with depression or some other emotion depends on their personal explanation for the loneliness (Peplau et al, 1982).

In summary, both loneliness *and* depression, although distinct experiences, can be viewed positively or negatively depending on how one defines each. It is perhaps obvious that if either interferes with effective human functioning, they are then deficits rather than stimuli to growth. These nuances require further research and theoretical frameworks.

Notions of aloneness and solitude are more subtle in relation to loneliness. Peter Suedfeld (1982) expresses this subtlety. "It is true that many people are alone; that many people feel lonely; and that some of those who are alone feel lonely" (p. 55). Fischer and Phillips (1982) found that adults living alone were less isolated from friends than those living with another person. As already noted, subjective well-being ("nonloneliness") is associated with the quality of relationship. Aloneness is not the same as loneliness (Lowenthal & Robinson, 1976).

Perhaps the most positive of the loneliness dimensions is that of solitude. It may be that the "self chosen for human growth" connotation of solitude takes away some of the onus from this concept as compared to "depression" or "aloneness." There seems little hope for growth in the midst of depression or aloneness. Not so in solitude.[6] Hartog (1980) sees the positiveness of solitude due to implicit *meaning* in the experience. Meaning carries a certain notion of control, of self choice that the depressed and the lonely seem to lack. Hartog's examples support this notion.

> Highly motivated hermits, martyrs, scientists, artists, and explorers usually handle their loneliness better than the abandoned, deserted, widowed, divorced because their lonely experience has meaning (p. 10).

Larson, Csikszentmihalyi, and Graef (1982) investigated the implications of "time alone." Their results support these concepts of control and meaning. Depending on individuals' resources (inner meaning), they will either find opportunities or limitations in a state of solitude. Fromm-Reichmann (1959) found that prisoners with meaning for their imprisonment (e.g., political prisoners) were best able to cope with and draw positively from solitary confinement. These observations have been supported by similar studies (Suedfeld, 1982). Peplau et al. (1982) report that "the explanations (meaning) people construct for their loneliness can influence the feelings and behaviors that accompany the experience of loneliness" (p. 135). Finally, cultural differences project solitude as a value; there is a creativity to be gained from solitude (Hartog, 1980). The Indian, the mystic, the artist, are all examples of individuals positively drawing from solitude. On the other hand, the crazed person emerging from *imposed* solitude dramatizes how different are the results of a freely chosen or imposed solitude.

III. Implications for the Religious Educator

The first implication derives from the complexity of the issue which in turn derives from the complexity of person. The complexity of person is further influenced by the reality that persons interact with each other within a given environment. That individuals are microcosms of the universe has often been a truism of philosophical discussion. It is, moreover, important that the religious educator be aware of the ramifications that these perspectives imply. First, simplistic platitudes in religious education are inappropriate. Educational ministry must fit the human condition. Humans are not simple. They are filled with paradox and surprise. Plans are aborted, dreams are stilled, and injustice emerges in different forms. Recognizing these contingencies and being able to "live" with them, the religious educator formulates new plans, fashions new dreams, and continues the fight for justice. If, as Chesterton tells us, we have not seriously "tried" to make Christianity work, perhaps we have oversimplified Augustine's "love God and do what you will."

A second ramification concerns control. For some, control is sinister, a characteristic of the powerful. But Jesus said, "I take up my life and I lay it down again." Control, in the sense used here, provides direction; it is a rudder which can move the person into the shoals as well as the harbor, but it demands purpose and commitment of the hand, heart, and head that guide it.

A third and final ramification of human complexity is the limitless possibilities that arise. The freedom to choose which "god" to call our own is an unalienable right and responsibility which religious educators cannot compromise. Urban Holmes (1979) sums up these initial assumptions when he says, "The openness of a contemporary person to God's word is made possible within the context of the world in which we live" (p. 76).

Therefore, to understand loneliness within religious education, it is necessary to pray *and* research. An ongoing dialogue between religion and the sciences can be fruitful and compelling if our human potential and that of our faith community is to be enhanced by the spirit of meaning and understanding.

The following reflections are based on the preceding discussion of loneliness research and on the imperative of religious education to understand its nuances. Jesus often retired to a place apart. Why? To pray? To recuperate? To mourn? To dream? All of these? Was he lonely, depressed, an isolate? What was the nature of his religious relationship? What is meant by a triune relationship of Father, Son, and Spirit?

Clearly, these are profound questions which each of us spends more than a lifetime investigating. I would suggest, however, that within the issue of loneliness (and its opposite, community) lies a substantial insight into the meaning of our faith which is the underlying motif of religious education. There are volumes of literature dealing with community. There are, on the other hand, very few works that hypothesize loneliness as a key to understanding relationship. After all, its link to relationship is as deficit. But perhaps the existentialists are privy to an understanding that, within a context of faith, could replicate the "aha" experience of psychology.

> Both loneliness and creativity contain a quality of anticipation and expectation. Perhaps it is a recapitulation of the child's awaiting the return of mother or the expectation that she will be there after the early tentative explorations end. The pregnant woman also is "expecting." It is as though the goal of a creative work was a regression to an earlier state of bliss or a moment of warm security, to be followed by a return to exploration and novelty seeking (Hartog, 1980; p. 24).

Yahweh says to the people of Israel, "I will wipe away every tear from your eyes." It seems that this promise can be metaphorically accomplished each time religious educators are able to replace loneliness with the hope and expectation of renewed life (relationship) within community. "What you do to the least of my people, you do to me."

The basis of this theory lies in a dual process. Persons are not only capable of 1) self-reflection on their own thoughts but also 2) reflection on the exigencies of the world about them. Building on a recognition that the lonely seem to have an external focus of control, it may be possible to diminish or eliminate loneliness by adjusting the locus of control toward an internal mode, if that is indeed an option. This process might be accomplished by looking at previous research. It has been found that the degree of loneliness may be dependent upon "personal resources."

> An important area for study would be the "personal resources" that enable individuals to stave off loneliness when social partners are not available, such as diaries, pets, person-

ality characteristics, attribution of responsibility for the partner's absence, and so forth (Derlega & Margulis, 1982; p. 161).

Preliminary results have indicated that those individuals with "personal resources" are less lonely than those without. An intervention strategy that has shown significant results is that of teaching social skills (Jones, Hobbs, & Hockenbury, in press). In this study, "the treatment group showed a significant reduction in loneliness between baseline and posttreatment assessments" (Peplau & Perlman, 1982; p. 249). By "equipping" the lonely with social skills, they may be sufficiently motivated to begin to shift their locus of control to a more internal mode.

A second strategy dealing with the influence of the environment on lonely individuals would be to help those individuals identify and maintain a support group that provides only affirming feedback. This group would "ensure" positive material out of which the individual might fashion a kind of "self-fulfilling prophecy." This dual approach is aimed at strengthening (or, if possible, actually shifting to) an internal locus of control.[7]

While this theory is sketched very briefly, possibilities of success do seem realizable. The following is a suggested research design.

H$_1$: Social skills development is unrelated to internal locus of control.

H$_2$: A support system is unrelated to an internal locus of control.

Design: An experimental and control group (drawn from individuals who have been evaluated on the UCLA Loneliness Scale and the I-E Instrument).

1. Parameters of a lonely and nonlonely person are defined prior to the testing time.

2. Experimental Group Treatment:
   a. Social skills development (approximately six months).
   b. Prior (to skill-development process) formulation of a support group for each member chosen by each member; periodic sessions with support group and treatment facilitator throughout the six months.
   c. Repeat of testing procedures.
   d. Debriefing of experimental and support groups.

Although the research design implies a specified time and procedure, the theory driving the research can be immediately operationalized in a number of ways. I will suggest a process of what I call, "loneliness discernment" that is integral and has, I believe, the potential to facilitate faith development. There are four steps in this process.

1. Recognize Assumptions

It is important that religious educators understand what prompts them to act (Rook and Peplau, 1982). It has been suggested that loneliness is difficult to recognize because its presence is an embarrassment or the emotion is simply too overwhelming to name. If religious educators are themselves uncomfortable with the experience, they may not be disposed to understand the experience in the lives of others. Robert S. Weiss (1973), noted for his work on loneliness, suggests,

> Working out how we came to have a capacity for loneliness may have no direct application, but it may increase our acceptance of loneliness as a response as natural—and as valuable—as hunger (p. 77).

Another author calls for finding an optimal range of human contact (Flanders, 1982). He says, "Too little human contact elicits poignant feelings of loneliness. Too much human contact produces social overload, a stressor that often afflicts psychologists and psychiatrists" (p. 171). How differently religious educators might approach loneliness from an assumption that it is as "natural as hunger" than one which sees loneliness as an evil or someone's "fault."

Religious educators might also be aware of the cultural basis for their perspective on loneliness. Are assumptions based on society's view of unsatisfying relationships as social failure? Is there compassion available that moves the educator toward helping the lonely enhance or even begin to develop social skills? Is there an awareness that the values of competition, uninvolvement, and independence—American values—are different and may conflict with basic human needs for community, engagement, and dependence on others (Slater, 1970)? Does a philosophy of "more is better" permeate assumptions regarding loneliness regardless of research that has consistently verified that quality and not quantity of relationship differentiates the lonely from the nonlonely?

In short, have religious educators done their "homework" before attempting to minister to the needs of others? "The point is that prescriptions for loneliness cures must be based on accurate diagnosis of the problems, rather than on cultural myths" (Rook and Peplau, 1982). Perhaps our assumptions need to be reassessed and adjusted for their integrity.

2. Identify Feelings

Religious educators must know how their faith community *feels*. The fact that a friend should not feel sad does not stop the friend's feeling sad. If the sadness is abated, it is probably due to the concern expressed rather than an intellectual process that repeats "I should not feel sad."

Feelings will give religious educators a measure of how serious the loneliness is. Religious educators might be better able to fashion a plan of intervention(s) if they use a schema such as Young's classification of chronic, situational, and transient loneliness. Feelings can be assessed as to intensity and duration. It is important to understand that loneliness is sometimes not recognized and named loneliness by the lonely.

> Often loneliness is not felt; instead the person has a feeling of unexplained dread, or desperation, or of extreme restlessness. The astute clinician must therefore be prepared to infer the presence of loneliness from other signs and cues. . . . Depression can be triggered by the sorts of changes in one's social realities that often lead to loneliness (e.g., divorce or widowhood), but depression can also result from nonsocial events (e.g., loss of one's job, flunking out of school, illness) that may be unrelated to loneliness (Rook & Peplau, 1982; p. 353).

Feelings also give some indication of the individual's locus of control. From where are the person's thought and actions coming? Is there a feeling that no individual effort can make a difference? What or who is the cause for happiness or unhappiness? This assessment of feelings obviously takes time, attention, and investment. Religious education is a commitment that takes time, attention, and investment.

3. Describe Self-Concept

Rollo May (1953) has said, "Every human being gets much of his sense of his own reality out of what others say to him or think about him" (p. 32). The importance of understanding persons' self-concept is finding their "level(s)" of expectation. What do they expect of themselves? Of others? What do they think others expect of them? This investigation may help educators understand the assumptions of others. A fine line exists between assumption and expectation. Peplau, Miceli, and Morasch (1982) speak of a discrepancy model of self-evaluation in which loneliness is examined from the insider's perspective, on how lonely persons perceive and evaluate their social life, not on how others might view it. In this view, loneliness is "a response to the perception that one's social relations fail to measure up to some internal yardstick" (p. 137). This view is also supported by DeJong-Gierveld, 1978; Lopata, 1969; and Perlman and Peplau, 1981. In other words, how do people decide they are lonely? What is the relationship between loneliness and expectation?

An unresolved question is how people choose reference groups or standards (Peplau et al, 1982; Fischer & Phillips, 1982). This is possibly outside the scope of interventions for the religious educator, but it serves as a reminder of the complexity of the issue. It also serves to highlight the importance of value formation and its attendant research.

Research has shown that unrealistic expectations may be the cause for loneliness (Zilboorg, 1938). As mentioned earlier, it is one possible reason given for the research findings that the old are generally not lonely; they have chosen to expect less and are satisfied with less. Other factors are certainly important, but the power of expectation warrants careful attention by educators. Most importantly, formulating and operating out of realistic expectations offers potential satisfaction.

4. Distinguish and Define

Although the previous steps are in a suggested order with "defining" as a final step, the process need not (and probably will not) occur in this manner. The only consideration that deserves some priority is the step sorting out assumptions. Since we often act out of our assumptions, it is important to initially spend time in identifying these.

Sadler and Johnson (1980) are explicit in the importance of naming an experience. "No realistic confrontation with loneliness is possible until the experience is identified, carefully diagnosed and accepted at face value" (p. 36). Considerable attention has already been given to differences between loneliness, depression, aloneness, solitude, and isolation. Diagnosing one and eliminating others is more than applying a definition to persons and their actions. The complexity and interrelatedness of factors should caution religious educators to great care in "labeling." Two popular descriptions of Jesus give two very different perceptions of the man. In one, Jesus is called "the solitary man"; in another he is "the man for all seasons." Which is a more accurate description? Perhaps both?

The value of "naming" is the facility it gives in selecting an appropriate intervention that may help alleviate the distress—if there is distress. For with isolation, solitude, and aloneness, there are distinct possibilities for new life and stronger relationships through an experience of separateness.

Clearly, there are caveats in implementing this suggested approach. There is the danger of the religious educator becoming "psychologist." The wisdom of educators is most obvious in their recognizing the limits of their own expertise. Individuals who are hostile, withdrawn, and negative may indeed be lonely; they may also require help beyond the educator's skill.

Conclusion

This chapter has looked at loneliness and suggested ways in which religious educators might approach the lonely. It is hoped that some extended understanding of the concept of loneliness was gained by the reader. For loneliness is elusive and defies the parameters that more exact sciences would like to impose. Perhaps its elusiveness serves its "purpose." As some have suggested, its experience may serve a positive function of drawing attention to a deficit that interferes with human growth. On the other hand, perhaps it calls on religious educators to discern the importance of community by experiencing separateness.

Whatever our perspective, it is an experience of emptiness. Emptiness connotes a potential for fullness. Some have suggested that solitude and aloneness are opportunities to actualize that potential. Depression, in this context, seems to lack opportunity and potential. There's a feeling of hopelessness. If there is any message that religious educators are to bring to people, it is a message of hope. "Have hope that your joy may be complete." The task of religious educators is to perceive emptiness and separateness and discern the ways in which emptiness might be filled and separateness healed.

The paradox is that community is sometimes experienced most in moments "alone," just as we can sometimes feel the beauty of the dawn only after the darkest of nights.

Religious educators have an opportunity to offer community and life. They can capture that opportunity by study, prayer, and discernment. "He who supplies seed for the sower and bread for the eater will provide in abundance; he will multiply the seed you sow and increase your generous yield" (2 Corinthians 9:10).

Notes

1. "Time" is basic to Flanders' theory. His formula for human contact emphasizes the critical "dimensions of time as it concerns both frequen-

cy of interaction occasions and duration of the dyadic relationship over months and years" (p. 172). He criticizes the lack of "personal resource exchange" possible on Sunday which is no longer the "day of rest" but a day of continuing business; he sees TV as limiting human contact. These adverse conditions, over time, are taking their toll on satisfactory relationships.

Although the cognitive therapy proposed by Young is a problem-solving treatment, it recognizes that loneliness seems to stem from "specific, habitual errors or deficits in thinking." In fact, his description of one type of loneliness as "chronic" assumes a historical context for a condition which, by reason of inaccurate thought processes, is continued.

2. At adolescence, when peer relationships take on meanings of status, it may be additionally difficult for individuals to admit to loneliness. Saying "I'm lonely" may carry loss of prestige and open possibilities of further alienation.

3. Lowenthal & Robinson (1976) have suggested that the old may experience loneliness when comparisons between past and present relationships are unfavorable.

4. Aloneness and solitude can be used interchangeably. Greta Garbo's, "I want to be alone," was probably a wish for the renewing possibility that solitude offers. The image of a "solitary figure" can denote both strength and weakness depending on its context. When these terms are used, it is best to probe the experience for the intended meaning.

5. From Young, "Loneliness, Depression and Cognitive Therapy: Theory and Application," in L. A. Peplau & D. Perlman (Eds.) *Loneliness: A Sourcebook of Current Theory, Research, and Therapy.* New York: John Wiley & Sons, 1982, pp. 392-5.

6. This internal control may be developed by insisting that individuals take responsibility for their own actions. Second, by reinforcing their *effective* decisions religious educators will be sending affirming messages that will prove supportive. A third technique is also fairly simple. The educator provides a model of faith in action. The positive results of social learning through modeling has been the subject of research (Bandura, 1977). Religious literature has included its own "modeling" concepts. Popularly written books such as *Teaching the Way* (Grassi, 1982) say in different ways what Jesus told his followers, "I am the Way, the Truth, and the Life." There is an implied assumption in these interventions, i.e., that the religious educator understand and operate out of an internal locus of control.

7. Peplau, Miceli, & Morasch (1982) have suggested that linguistic categories and folk beliefs affect the individual's experience of loneliness and should be considered as a possible negative or positive source of self-fulfilling prophecies (p. 137).

References

Bandura, A. *Social learning theory*. Englewood Cliffs, N.J.: Prentice-Hall, 1977.

Beck, A. T. *Cognitive therapy and the emotional disorders*. New York: International Universities Press, 1976.

Bragg, M. *A comparative study of loneliness and depression*. Doctoral dissertation, University of California, Los Angeles, 1979.

Brennan, T. & Auslander, N. Adolescent loneliness: An exploratory study of social and psychological predispositions and theory. Unpublished manuscript, Behavioral Research Institute, Boulder Colo., 1979.

Cutrona, C. E. Theoretical approaches to loneliness. In L. A. Peplau & D. Perlman (Eds.), *Loneliness: A source book of current theory, research, and therapy*. New York: John Wiley & Sons, 1982.

Cutrona, C. E. & Peplau, L. A. A longitudinal study of loneliness. Paper presented at the annual meeting of the Western Psychological Association, San Diego, Calif., April 1979.

DeJong, J. & Raadschelders, J. Types of loneliness. In L. A. Peplau & D. Perlman (Eds.), *Loneliness: A source book of current theory, research, and therapy*. New York: John Wiley and Sons, 1982.

Derlega, V. J., & Grzelak, J. Appropriateness of self-disclosure in social relationships. *Journal of Social Issues*, 1977, 33(3), 102-115.

Derlega, V. J., & Margulis, S. T. Why loneliness occurs: The interrelationship of social-psychological and privacy concepts. In L. A. Peplau & D. Perlman (Eds.), *Loneliness: A sourcebook of current theory, research, and therapy*. New York: John Wiley & Sons, 1982.

Dyer, B. M. Loneliness—There's no way to escape it. *Alpha Gamma Delta Quarterly*, Spring 1974, 2-5.

Fischer, C. S. & Phillips, S. L., Who is alone? Social characteristics of people with small networks. In L. A. Peplau & D. Perlman (Eds.), *Loneliness: A sourcebook of current theory, research, and therapy*. New York: John Wiley & Sons, 1982.

Flanders, J. P. A general systems approach to loneliness. In L. A. Peplau & D. Perlman (Eds.), *Loneliness: A sourcebook of current theory, research, and therapy*. New York: John Wiley & Sons, 1982.

Fromm-Reichmann, F. Loneliness. *Psychiatry*, 1959, 22, 1-15.

Goswick, R. A., & Jones, W. H. Loneliness, self-concept, and adjustment. *Journal of Psychology*, 1981, 107, 237-240.

Haas-Hawkings, G. Intimacy as a moderating influence in the stress of loneliness in widowhood. *Essence*, 1978, 2(4), 249-258.

Hartog, J. The anlage and ontogeny of loneliness. In J. Hartog, J. R. Audy, & Y. A. Cohen (Eds.), *The anatomy of loneliness*. New York: International Universities Press, 1980.

Holmes, U. *Ministry and imagination*. Minneapolis, Minn.: Seabury, 1979.

Horowitz, L. M., & French, R. de S. Interpersonal problems of people who describe themselves as lonely. *Journal of Consulting and Clinical Psychology*, 1979, 47(4), 762-764.

Horowitz, L. M., French, R. de S., & Anderson, C. A. The prototype of a lonely person. In L. A. Peplau & D. Perlman (Eds.), *Loneliness: A sourcebook of current theory, research, and therapy*. New York: John Wiley & Sons, 1982.

Jones. W. H. Loneliness and social behavior. In L. A. Peplau & D. Perlman (Eds.), *Loneliness: A sourcebook of current theory, research, and therapy*. New York: John Wiley & Sons, 1982.

Larson, R, Csikszentmihalyi, M., & Graef, R. Time alone in daily experience: Loneliness or renewal? In L. A. Peplau & D. Perlman (Eds.), *Loneliness: A sourcebook of current theory, research, and therapy*. New York: John Wiley & Sons, 1982.

Lederer, W. J., & Jackson, D. D. False assumption 6: That loneliness will be cured by marriage. *The mirages of marriage*. New York: Norton, 1968.

Lopata, H. Z. Loneliness: Forms and components. *Social Problems*, 1969, 17, 248-261.

Lopata, H. Z., Heinemann, G. D., & Baum, J. Loneliness: Antecedents and coping strategies in the lives of widows. In L. A. Peplau & D. Perlman (Eds.), *Loneliness: A sourcebook of theory, research, and therapy*. New York: John Wiley & Sons, 1982.

Lowenthal, M. F., Thurner, M., & Chiriboga, D. *Four stages of life*. San Francisco: Jossey-Bass, 1976.

Lowenthal, M., & Robinson, B. Social networks and isolation. In R. Binstock & E. Shanas (Eds.), *Handbook of aging and the social sciences*. New York: Van Nostrand Reinhold, 1976.

May, R. The loneliness and anxiety of modern man. *Man's search for himself*. New York: Norton, 1953.

McCallister, L. & Fischer, C. S. A. A method for surveying personal networks. *Sociological Methods and Research*, 1978, 7, 131-148.

Mijuskovic, B. Loneliness: An interdisciplinary approach. In J. Hartog, J. R. Audy, & Y. A. Cohen (Eds.), *The anatomy of loneliness*. New York: International Universities Press, 1980.

Moustakas, C. E. *Loneliness*. New York: Prentice-Hall, 1961.

Paloutzian, R. F. & Ellison, D. W. Loneliness, spiritual wellbeing, and the quality of life. In L. A. Peplau & D. Perlman (Eds.), *Loneliness: A sourcebook of current theory, research, and therapy*. New York: John Wiley & Sons, 1982.

Peplau, L. A., Bikson, T. K., Rook, K. S., & Goodchilds, J. D. Being old and living alone. In L. A. Peplau & D. Perlman (Eds.), *Loneliness: A sourcebook of current theory, research, and therapy.* New York: John Wiley & Sons, 1982.

Peplau, L. A., Miceli, M., & Morasch, B. Loneliness and self-evaluation. In L. A. Peplau & D. Perlman (Eds.), *Loneliness: A sourcebook of current theory, research, and therapy.* New York: John Wiley & Sons, 1982.

Peplau, L. A. & Perlman, D. Perspectives on loneliness. In L. A. Peplau & D. Perlman (Eds.), *Loneliness: A sourcebook of current theory, research, and therapy.* New York: John Wiley & Sons, 1982.

Perlman, D. & Peplau, L. A. Theoretical approaches to loneliness. In L. A. Peplau & D. Perlman (Eds.), *Loneliness: A sourcebook of current theory, research, and therapy.* New York: John Wiley & Sons, 1982.

Perlman, D., & Peplau, L. A. Toward a social psychology of loneliness. In S. Duck & R. Gilmour (Eds.), *Personal relationships 3: Personal relationships in disorder.* London: Academic Press, 1981.

Rook, K. S. & Peplau, L. A. Perspectives on helping the lonely. In L. A. Peplau & D. Perlman (Eds.), *Loneliness: A sourcebook of current theory, research, and therapy.* New York: John Wiley & Sons, 1982.

Rubenstein, C. M. & Shaver, P. The experience of loneliness. In L. A. Peplau & D. Perlman (Eds.), *Loneliness: A sourcebook of current theory, research, and therapy.* New York: John Wiley & Sons, 1982.

Russell, D. The measurement of loneliness. In L. A. Peplau & D. Perlman (Eds.), *Loneliness: A sourcebook of current theory, research, and therapy.* New York: John Wiley & Sons, 1982.

Sadler, W. A. & Johnson, T. B. From loneliness to anomie. In J. Hartog, J. R. Audy, & Y. A. Cohen (Eds.), *The anatomy of loneliness.* New York: International Universities Press, 1980.

Shaver, P., & Rubenstein, C. Childhood attachment experience and adult loneliness. In L. Wheeler (Ed.), *Review of personality and social psychology* (Vol. 1). Beverly Hills, Calif.: Sage, 1980.

Slater, P. *The pursuit of loneliness: American culture at the breaking point.* Boston: Beacon Press, 1970.

Suedfled, P. Aloneness as a healing experience. In L. A. Peplau & D. Perlman (Eds.), *Loneliness: A sourcebook of current theory, research, and therapy.* New York: John Wiley & Sons, 1982.

Sullivan, H. S. *The interpersonal theory of psychiatry.* New York: Norton, 1953.

Tunstall, J. *Old and alone.* New York: Humanities Press, Inc., 1967.

Weiss, R. S. *Loneliness: The experience of emotional and social isolation.* Cambridge, Mass.: MIT Press, 1973.

Weiss, R. S. Issues in the study of loneliness. In L. A. Peplau & D. Perlman (Eds.), *Loneliness: A sourcebook of current theory, research, and therapy.* New York: John Wiley & Sons, 1982.

Young, J. E. Loneliness, depression, and cognitive therapy: Theory and application. In L. A. Peplau & D. Perlman (Eds.), *Loneliness: A source-*

book of current theory, research, and therapy. New York: John Wiley & Sons, 1982.

Zilboorg, G. Loneliness. *Atlantic Monthly,* January 1938, 45-54.

Zimbardo, P. G. *Psychology and life,* 10th ed. Glenview, Ill.: Scott Foresman, 1979.

Chapter 2

The Life Cycle and Loneliness

You can read it daily in some magazine or paper: The breakdown of the family and the collapse of marriage commitment is the cause of loneliness today! Other critics blame it on unemployment, increased job mobility, and "current lack of faith." Everyone, it seems is looking for someone or something to blame. When we examine these arguments empirically, however, it appears that, in many substantial ways, the more things have changed, the more they have remained the same. It turns out that the "good old days" were just as fraught with problems and crises as any other period in history. Folk wisdom may not always be so wise. Recent statistics indicate that, for example, people are taking good care of the elderly within their own home now more than ever. Other research produced by the University of Hawaii argued that, according to their sample, individuals in the country were less likely than city dwellers to respond to someone in trouble. Perhaps we have missed the boat on this, and it would be more useful to examine human nature and experience more closely to see how the human person develops throughout the life cycle, with particular attention to loneliness. We might then emerge with a more appropriate developmental context within which to understand the problem of loneliness. It seems that the human person experiences loneliness in a myriad of contexts throughout the life cycle. In fact, it seems that each age brings with it its own particular brand of loneliness. The remaining chapters of this book will explore each major segment of the life cycle and see how loneliness is experienced and dealt with at each juncture.

The Life Cycle: An Overview

For want of a better vocabulary, the human person seems born with an innate set of needs and expectations which are a combination of genetics, evolution, and social development. As the individual experiences these needs and expectations and has them met and/or frustrated an entire sequence of "further options" begins to fall into place. For example, if children are never responded to positively when they cry or need something, it is clear that shortly they learn there is no sense in crying since "who is there to listen?" The disastrous results which occur when children begin making choices regarding their options later in life are testified to in abundance in the clinical and increasingly in religious development literature. Need and expectation, like memory and hope, form the balance points of all individuals during their lives and will pattern their later abilities in some substantial way.

Infancy and Childhood

The experience of loneliness apparently begins in infancy and is referred to in the clinical literature as "separation anxiety." The term describes the reaction of the infant when he or she is temporarily separated from the primary caretaker. When infants are separated from their caretakers they become agitated, upset, and depressed. It would appear that this first experience is prototypical and forms the foundation for all later reactions to coping with separation and loss. This negative reaction can be significantly reduced when the child has *multiple* caretakers who share the responsibility for maintenance and care as well as love. There have been empirical indications that a child functions well with up to ten caretakers. It would appear that, even from the beginning, there is a *communal* aspect to the child's development. It is immediately obvious that the communal nature of the church's mission as well as its calling to shared responsibility might provide a natural teaching ground for individuals to cope with and integrate their feelings of loneliness and separateness. Community will not magically transform an individual's problems, but it does give the person an opportunity to address the problems within a supportive context.

Community seems a natural remedy but, at least in the United States, there is a deep cultural emphasis on competition (Natale, 1973). This competitive atmosphere increases the risk of isolation and loneliness because the fact of competition implies an inability to share common goals since personal success might be jeopardized by sharing with the competitor who could, in turn, "win" over you (Natale, 1978).

The cultural emphasis on competition is exacerbated by the increasing number of people who divorce rather than stay in unsatisfactory relationships. *Whatever the reasons for a divorce,* children tend to blame themselves, and this experience of "being the blame" for the divorce can shatter a child's self-confidence. Obviously, people will not stay together in intolerable relationships only to avoid the child's problems. It is critical, however, for the parents to be able to put aside their own problems and to help children deal with the feeling that the marriage breakup was their own fault.

Along with the shift in family/intimacy patterns, the increasing career moves which characterize especially middle-class families reduce the child's ability to make sustaining friendships. Teachers and religious educators need to be especially sensitive to children who join the community as well as those who spend time with imaginary friends or who have clear (or subtle) problems in making real friendships. Here it is also important that the teacher and religious educator emphasize the difference between being alone and lonely. Loneliness and being alone are not the same thing and children need to be challenged and encouraged to explore many of the things which they can achieve on their own in terms of hobbies, prayer, reflection, self-searching, etc. In fact, the interaction effect of solitude-interaction can be a major teaching tool for teachers anxious to communicate genuine religious education. Religious development requires *both* solitude and interaction. The child who can never be alone is in equally dangerous straits as the child who cannot successfully bond with others. Balance between individual integrity and individuation with community and society is the goal.

The precarious tasks of childhood completed, the young adolescent faces further challenges to personal growth. The adolescent finds that the primary psychological needs for tenderness and acceptance which characterized the early years are augmented by the desire for intimacy. This *requires* the development of friendships. The adolescent without some close friends faces an acute situation of loneliness. Adolescence is characterized by the need to develop a personal and unique identity. This task, without which there would be no personality integration, is made all the more difficult by the unrealistically high expectations placed before adolescents today in the media. Families, churches, educational institutions, as well as television and magazines, parade a series of high expectations about what life *ought* to be like and what an "ordinary" life should entail.

The agony of adolescent loneliness is evident on weekend evenings—traditionally the peak period for isolated feelings and complaints about being lonely.

The religious/moral educator may effectively intervene here with group and individual experiences and interactions as well as cognitive training which is aimed at correcting the adolescent's social expectations. Rath's value analyses have proven invaluable in enabling adolescents to understand the discrepancy between what the media and social pressure promise and what is a realistic analysis of human nature and experience. Through a deft cognitive training in expectation analysis and a realistic goal to achieve many adolescents can move effectively into a non-cynical, positive appreciation of human relationships.

Young adulthood, a period roughly similar to the time when many people are college students, is a critical time when students/individuals often make the friendships which are to last a lifetime. Interestingly, young adults often report that transitory relationships only increase a sense of loneliness, and it is untrue that most young adults have no positive moral and religious values. It is also at this time that young adults experience in a more obvious way the two major types of isolation: *Emotional* isolation caused by the absence of key figures in their lives and *social* isolation caused by an absence of a network of friends.

Often the approach most useful for the moral and religious educator at this time when so many young people are questioning their heritage and values is to enter into the exploration *with* them. Within the community context, the individuals can explore and refine their social skills as well as work at improving their self concepts. It is critical that the individual become involved in a religious education which conforms to our state of art information about human growth and development. The religious organization with its emphasis on community is in an ideal position to aid the young adult during this time.

To aid in the development of the youth's positive self-concept it is crucial that the program in religious education be one which is structured along positive cognitive lines (of James Michael Lee) and that the young adult have the opportunity to explore his/her skills within the concept of an affirming community. Often young adults have a "conversion" experience which is more hysteria and defense against social isolation than anything genuinely ascribable as religious development. Genuine religious conversion *can* be explored as any other phenomenon without doing damage to anyone.

Young adulthood is a period of life during which many people move into a committed, monogamous relationship. For many people, this is marriage. Men and women diverge greatly during this time in the life cycle. Over and over again the research indicates that married men are least likely to be lonely while single men are most likely to experience loneliness. Married women, on the other hand, are most likely to experience depression during this period of their lives. This is often connected with having children. The woman experiences herself (realistically) as deprived of adult company while the husband's daily schedule remains essentially unaffected by parenthood.

Generally, the polls indicate that individuals are less satisfied with marriage during this period of their lives than any other. The divorce figures substantiate this.

Men do not escape the loneliness trap, however. This is a time in life when men (and women who choose not to marry) find it most difficult to make friends in the workplace since co-workers are often perceived as *competitors*. It is, hence, difficult to make the necessary links between people. Competition destroys cooperation. The price: Work is a dangerous arena for gladiatorial combat. Even when workers appear cooperative, the threat of relocation is so great today that intimacy seems pointless.

The divorce rates are also highest during this time in the life cycle—with the concomitant dose of loneliness. However, it is significant to note that, apparently, this loneliness is situational and transitional since half of all divorced people remarry within a year.

Midlife

While many authors have bemoaned the midlife crisis, it is apparently *not* a period of great loneliness. In fact, people seem busier at this time than at any other time in their lives. The multiple demands of both generations (parents and children) seem to involve the mid-life person continually in action directed at problem solving.

This is also a time when, at least in our research, religious commitment is beginning to reformulate itself in distinctly personal terms. The combination of hectic time schedules, extensive emotional demands, and a more expansive understanding of religious development appear to vitiate the effects of loneliness on individuals.

Many myths about midlife seem to be changing. For example, there appears to be little evidence of "the empty nest syndrome." With the increased personal freedom brought on by the departure of the children, individuals in midlife seem to be busy. In fact, when surveyed, virtually 50 percent of the men and 35 percent of the women claimed that they had no friends. It is clear that this truce between loneliness and the individual is only temporary and a healthy adult must find more productive ways of handling it.

Religious education offers a distinctive approach to individuals during this time of life. Correct education can, for example, help individuals map out a life path based on an understanding of who the person is *and* self-transcendence. This is not a time for indoctrination (frankly, one can imagine no appropriate time for manipulation of this sort). This is a time for exploration. Values, attitudes, needs, and expectations need to be laid out and compared against what one's sense of transcendence is and means. There is nothing more sad than a supposed adult acting out his/her life based on *someone else's* commitment. Clearly, the religious educator can enable individuals to explore their own sense of transcendence, connect this to a sense of community, and finally articulate this in action. This is, in short, a time in life when one must integrate individual needs for ascendancy with a sense of corporate involvement and communal concern. We are not simply individuals.

Mature Years

Midlife leads into the mature years (55+). Individuals begin to experience for the first time in their lives that there is more time behind them than ahead of them. Life begins to give intimations of mortality signaled by the chronic illnesses and death of friends and family. One begins to look toward retirement. There is a certain existential loneliness reported by most adults interviewed, but all quickly added that there were considerable compensations as well. Notable among the rewards is that the fifties are seen today as a vibrant period of living. Many individuals also enjoyed the grandchildren—without the concomitant responsibility. Men begin to gain friends at work as they mentor younger colleagues while at home these men make friends with older men who are available because of their retirement.

Women responded differently and reported being considerably less satisfied with their husbands than their husbands were with them. Divorce rates are, however, low at this period of life.

Here the religious educator may call upon his/her understanding of the life cycle and evoke the generativity in individuals at this age. It is this age group that will incarnate the notion of community.

Retirement

Men report that they are three times more lonely in retirement than they were earlier in their lives. The two predominating causes of loneliness in old age are the loss of spouse and isolation from friends. Nothing can be done about the loss of spouse, but one *can* remain close and in contact of some sort with friends. This is critical, and it should be clear by now from the research that an old person living with relatives and distant from their surroundings and friends will be *more* lonely than someone living on their own but in an environment they can understand and with which they can feel bonded.

Loneliness in old age poses a particular problem for women who tend to live longer. The role of developing intimacy/support networks cannot be overemphasized for people at all ages—and especially for the old person. The church can and ought to play a crucial role here with its natural proclivity for gatherings, etc. The religious educator may often have to go to the people who are older to bring them into the community. Needless to say, the religious educator must be prepared to help individuals explore questions of ultimate meaning at this transitional stage of living. One often finds that doctrine and orthodoxy give way to a clear, committed, incarnated, and affectively bonded vision of transcendence.

It is clear that loneliness permeates the human condition and manifests itself differently throughout the life cycle. How does one intervene in helping individuals cope with the problems they face?

No one encounters this situation more acutely than the educator and none more starkly than the religious educator. People turn to the religious educator for answers to questions that other teachers are not expected to be able to approach. What are they to do?

A survey of the recent religious education materials suggests that scant attention has been given to the problem of loneliness from an empirical point of view. The religious materials border on the silly and authors fall over their own inferential logic, more concerned, it appears, with promoting dogma than exploring the implications of a valid human experience.

The answer, I believe, will come in part from the social sciences with their emphasis on *empirical* research. This has been the thrust of a handful of empirically oriented research educators in religion, among them James Michael Lee of the University of Alabama at Birmingham and John Wilson, fellow of Mansfield College, Oxford. They have individually laid the groundwork in their own areas of competence for the kind of research upon which this book is based.

References

Bolea, A. Loneliness in children. *The Psychotherapy Patient,* 1986, 2 (4).

Natale, S. M. Adolescent identity in secondary education. In Michael Warren (Ed.), *Resources for youth.* New York: Paulist Press, 1978.

Natale, S. M. The lonely patient. *The Psychotherapy Patient,* 1986, 2 (4).

Wilson, J. B. & Natale, S. M. First steps in moral education. *Thought,* 1985, 60, 237.

Chapter 3

Loneliness in Infancy and Childhood

An essential question to begin with here is exactly when do young people initially experience loneliness. Many people feel that loneliness first occurs when children are forced to stay in their own rooms at night when they have a clear-cut fear of the darkness. Many feel that children initially become lonely when they are lost or separated from a parent. However, it seems apparent that children actually experience loneliness initially at the moment they leave their mother's womb—in other words, even before they are conscious of their feelings.

Of course the children are not actually cognizant that it is *loneliness* they are experiencing, since they have not really cognitively grasped the various distinctions between love and hate, acceptance and nonacceptance, etc. However, within their psyches the children are already registering affective sensations of pleasure and pain, comfort and discomfort.

The great psychotherapist Otto Rank (1973) was so impressed by the consequences of childbirth trauma that he formulated his entire counseling procedure around it. He stated that in analysis the patient is really struggling for a rebirth, for a new entry into a world that does not possess the complications of life entailed in the first entry. So, says

Rank, the patient unconsciously associates personal problems with the original upheaval and displacement from the womb's protection (pp. 4-5).

The suggestion is that loneliness in children is ontological and is closely connected with their beings from the very moment of their birth. The latter has physiological and neurological aspects which cannot be totally erased. So, despite excellent treatment of children or the love of their parents they will continue throughout their lives to experience personal anxieties and uncertainties which are related to the shock of childbirth.

What must take the place of the womb's security for any child is gentle cradling and physical assurance by the parent(s). As Ashley Montagu has pointed out, what the newborn child has a basic right to expect is a continuation of the peaceful life experienced in the uterus. If this does not take place, severe trauma and incipient loneliness can be implanted.

Many writers in recent years have made vital studies of the attachment and separation patterns in young children's lives. What all of these studies suggest is that the small child can be attached to one figure, the mother or an adequate mother-surrogate, more than to any others in its life. Depriving the child of this figure, especially during the child's first three years, can possibly lead to serious psychological maladjustments not only in childhood but also throughout life.

For example, even brief separations from a parent can upset a young child by way of *protest* or by *despair*. If the mother, for example, does not return, despair can lead to *detachment,* a form of emotional self-protection roughly equivalent to an adult's decision not to expect anything so as not to be disappointed. If the mother returns within a reasonable length of time and the young child can resume attachment, then detachment can be abandoned. However, if these periods are prolonged the child may possibly assume a permanent stance of detachment and despair over the prospect of achieving a permanent relationship.

Now, the basic importance in understanding the attachment between the parent, the primary caregiver, and the infant in our discussion of loneliness is clearly its relationship to the ability of an individual to form close and satisfying attachments later in life. Infants, for example, who demonstrate strong attachments to their mothers also demonstrate capabilities of forming strong ties to others in their environment, such as peers, siblings, and other significant adults. Indeed, an effective mother-infant bond has been posited as a basic prerequisite for healthy emotional growth, and Freud asserted that the dynamics of the relationship between mother and infant set the stage for virtually all subsequent social interactions, and psychoanalytic theory bases many of its assertions and treatments on the important of the *mother-infant* dyad.

Children who, due to extreme circumstances, become separated from their mothers between the ages of six months and three years go through a series of reactions from intense rage to despair. One can usually observe unhealthy behavior in infants whose mothers have an abnormal lack of responsiveness to their needs.

After the age of three children tend to experience less distress when they are left by the major parent. (This age corresponds nicely with the nearly full development of the human brain.) However, it is impossible to assess the extent of the damage done to a tender psyche as a result of being left alone by the mother or mother-surrogate. The feelings of despair which many commentators have described may lead to a more or less permanent state of anxiety or to a sense of personal rejection which not even psychoanalysis can overcome.

The basic need for touching and stroking does not end

when the plateau of independence has been reached after the age of three. Indeed, the need continues for years, and in some children it never abates. Touching and cradling continue to be important nonverbal symbols capable of recalling and reconstituting the feelings of security which the children experience as babies in their mother's womb and later in their arms. If these basic symbols cease before the children are prepared, then anxiety and loneliness are bound to follow. Consequently, many adults are troubled by a sense of loneliness or rejection which owes more to childhood deprivation than to anything which happens to them in the adult world. Thus children who suffer become adults who suffer.

Bruno Bettelheim (1975) has observed that "there is no greater threat in life than that we will be deserted, left all alone . . . man's greatest fear . . . (is) separation anxiety" (p. 15). Bettelheim constantly emphasizes the connection between childhood fears and continuing apprehension in childhood. Separation anxiety, he notes, is hardly restricted to a particular period of development. However, since separation anxiety is clearly a basic component of loneliness in children, let us focus on it in some detail and depth.

Freud has stated that *darkness* and *separation anxiety* are prime contributors to loneliness. Separation from a meaningful adult is what matters, not the phobia of the thing in itself. What clearly frightens a child is to be separated from the mother or other important adult, and darkness, loneliness, and other anxiety-producing experiences become metaphors for this basic phobia. In fact, Freud even insisted that every adult phobia could be traced to a childhood anxiety.

An important statistic to mention here is that in the United States over half the mothers with school-age children and one-third the mothers with preschool-age children are employed outside the home. There is little won-der then that psychologists are worried about the phenom-enon of the "empty house" and what it will do to present generations of infants and children. The empty house is viewed as a symbol of separation anxiety of children, one which untimately amplifies all feelings of loneliness and parental rejection which they may have experienced from other causes.

As John Bowlby (1973) notes, "Young children are upset by even brief separations. Older children are upset by longer ones. Adults are upset whenever a separation is prolonged or permanent as in bereavement" (p. 10). The point here is that to a young child who is as yet inexperi-enced about worldly matters even a short separation may seem permanent, an actual bereavement. Gradually the child learns better and is able to endure separations more stoically, realizing that they will pass.

However, some children actually come to identify *separation with death* out of fear that the meaningful parent will die when they are apart. Consider the case, for example, of a small child who is convinced that her mother's death may occur while she is in school simply due to the fact that this mother is older than her friends' mothers.

However, even if children do distinguish between separa-tion and actual death, they may continue to regard any threat of separation as though it were permanent. For ex-ample, this might be true when the threat possibly involves unknown factors with which the children are not experi-enced, such as a threat to bring in an outsider to remove the child from the scene.

Bowlby feels that of even greater consequence in dis-turbing the child is a threat to abandon the child, for the child fears separation even more than the loss of love. Though parents may seldom mean such a threat when they use it and it may possibly be a form of teasing, albeit a cruel one, children certainly have no way of realizing this. To children the threats may be quite real, and a particularly rebellious child may even defy a parent regarding the threat.

Occasionally children must be left with relatives or friends, and if the children are loved and well cared for, and if sufficient preparation is made for them, such occasions should not be traumatic and cause for feelings of loneliness. However, children often remember these occasions with great uneasiness, and children who have never been properly fondled and loved as infants or as very young children often recall these occasions with enormous anxiety.

Probably the greatest single problem of separation anxiety with children usually occurs when children must begin their formal educational experience outside the home. This can be a very traumatic experience for many children; it certainly represents a major alteration in every child's lifestyle. As Martin Herbert (1975) has pointed out, "During these hours there is no appeal to mother's protection and comfort; the mantle of authority has been handed over to strangers" (p. 133).

Many teachers suggest that children experience separation anxiety to the greatest degree when they are first sent to school at ages four to six. When children become more familiar with a school's routines, they become less anxious. However, there is often another wave of anxiety around age eight when there is usually a heightened level of expectation which requires more difficult work of children in the third and fourth grade.

As children proceed through the educational system, they often discover that teachers are more interested in programing than in educating. The educational system and process often produces a feeling of alienation in many students; this latter feeling coupled with a feeling that school is a boring experience has a relationship to children's loneliness that should be quite obvious. To the extent that school can drive a wedge between their energy and the desire to learn and drug their natural curiosity, this divorces children from a world of excitement that would counterbalance their sense of being alone.

If children are unduly pushed to achieve good grades, or if they fail to achieve these grades, they may be left with the consolation that their parents will love them because of the push for the grades achieved.

Psychologist John Gottman of the University of Illinois has studied the problem of students' fears and loneliness and thinks that one major reason for unhappiness is simple *shyness*. Coming from homes where they have been able to retreat from difficulties instead of facing them, they are clearly ill at ease in social situations which involve confrontation, especially with large numbers of other children. Many of these students hover on the crowd's edge or withdraw from active participation with other students. Bullies easily spot such "hoverers" and intimidate them.

Children who have physical handicaps, speech problems, or obvious physical or behavioral peculiarities are easy targets for teasing by other children. Thus, nicknames and epithets like Skinny, Fatty, Four Eyes, and Peewee are quite common in most schools. However, thoughtful parents usually try to shield their children from the unpleasantness associated with physical differences.

Nevertheless, tender, sensitive children are targets of their peers, especially if their sensitivity involves any type of weakness. Sometimes it is not only the poor student, physically or mentally, who is punished and abused by other children, but also it can be the exceptionally good student who is noticed and rewarded by his teachers for being bright or dedicated.

A type of child who is a candidate for loneliness is the one who has a physical handicap associated with unattractiveness, such as skin diseases, overly prominent birthmarks, crippled or amputated limbs, and those prone to epileptic seizures.

In recent years psychological research has indeed given credence to the concerns people feel about looking good to other people. For example, many researchers have produced evidence to show that attractive people are usually evaluated as doing better work than people who are less good-looking, even though both groups' accomplishments are the same. Good-looking people are almost always preferred over unattractive ones in hiring for jobs, and teachers frequently favor good-looking students over less good-looking ones.

More than one psychologist has noted that the formation of identity is the chief work of children in their adolescent period. And identity formation depends largely on how adolescents perceive that they are being seen by the world around them. However, identity is not arrived at in a vacuum; identity is what emerges from a person's readings of other people's responses to his or her way of looking and behaving and speaking in their midst. This involves feedback and monitoring of the feedback.

In many children this process is a quite delicate one. If early family rearing has not already carefully socialized them and given them a strong sense of identity, they place great weight on the feedback they receive from persons outside the family, especially their peers and teachers. If children do not receive the sort of care and attention they wish through normal social means, they might even report to antisocial behavior or retreat into their own lonely shell.

Ideally, of course, what all children seek is confirmation from others that they are beautiful, good, and intelligent.

It is not really beneficial to lie to children about their appearance, but it is important to encourage them within all the boundaries of absolute truthfulness to set their qualities in the best possible light so that they are constantly in touch with the best that is in them. Self-image is frequently the only guide a child has for the future; therefore, the greatest care should be taken by all adults in order to aid children to perceive themselves in the best possible light.

It seems incredible to note that so much research should be done on the psychology of childhood, and so many important books written about it, but there has not really been established in the schools from the third grade upward seminars and courses in psychological factors which shape students' lives. It relieves children's inner pressures to understand something of the developmental process by which they respond to their environment and form personalities. Possessing the language with which to think and speak about the process would enable children to cope with it much more effectively than they can when it is proceeding as mere subliminal pain and pressure in their existence.

One psychological factor which definitely appears to shape children's minds is *mobility*—the American family's penchant for moving from place to place. As Alvin Toffler (1971) has indicated, "never have men's relationships, with place been more numerous, fragile, and temporary" (p. 75).

The average American family moves so many times in its lifetime that the very conception of the nature of a home has changed. For centuries prior to this one there was a human commitment to place, to property, to land, but this does not appear to be the case today with the dreary sameness which characterizes most houses. Property appears to be expendable and interchangeable, and this does not allow the sort of time—years and years—that are necessary to become rooted in a place, to know neighbors and make friends, to establish relationships, to make a bond with the land.

What must be emphasized is that when a person moves, he leaves his entire system behind, with the exception of selected possessions and family members. One's nervous system must accommodate itself to new response patterns, a new house and neighborhood, new personalities with respect to teachers and classmates, even to subtle emotional changes in parents who may also be undergoing stress. One actually grieves for items that have passed out of one's life and it is as though a part of one's life has died and everything in it as well. The child who is uprooted and removed from precious inanimate objects (like benches, swings, buildings, etc.) misses them in much the same way that an adult would miss a friend or neighbor.

For example, leaving loved toys behind can have a very negative effect on children. Also, children are often forced to leave animals, beloved family pets, behind when they move.

However, it is not merely missing friends and possessions that makes moving to another home so difficult for children. There is also the significant problem involved in adjusting to new patterns of existence at the other end of the move. Consequently, even children who appear relatively calm and placid about leaving a previous home can encounter much anxiety while they learn to live in a new home.

Bowlby is one of the many writers who support the belief that people enjoy advantages by remaining in familiar environments. Clearly, the physio-chemical systems that mediate attachment behavior and fear behavior operate much more favorably within a recognized and carefully defined section of the environment. When one leaves the boundaries of familiar territory, one more than likely excites stress mechanisms and gives rise to stress anxiety. Bowlby and many other writers feel that there is even a strong genetic bias in behalf of certain places and territories; overriding this produces undue tension and loneliness in a person.

Death and Loneliness

Maria Nagy (1959, p. 56) concludes after a perceptive study of almost four hundred children that those under five have very little conception of what it means to die, children learn enough about death between ages five to nine to be afraid of it, and at ages ten or eleven they begin to understand death in terms of its reality. At this point children begin to understand death most fully and to fear that it is something which can indeed occur to them. It is *after* this age that children appear to develop such a complete control of death's concept that they can describe it biologically and logically.

But what is important for adults to perceive is that even very small children can become deeply upset by images of death; this may occur through the death of a pet, or a human being, or a death witnessed in a television show. Fear of separation, quite naturally present in a child, becomes greatly enlarged by a death encounter, and the very fact that death is still somewhat poorly defined in the child's mind gives it a pervasive power and permeates the child's thinking.

Parents simply do not realize how anxious and frightened children can be about death. One way for a parent to be familiar with this is through the aforementioned death of a favorite pet; then the parent can engage the child in a dialogue about the meaning and significance of what has occurred.

Childhood, of course, or very early adolescence is the period when children focus most carefully on the formation of their identities. If the threat of dying, or simply the very topic of dying is introduced into the general scheme of things, this can become very upsetting to the child. A child might be far too likely to read too much into the slightest physical difficulty he/she is encountering, or the child may focus on a death example and see himself/herself dying in a similar manner.

Obviously, children simply do not have the emotional maturity to cope with an intellectual understanding of death in their early or late childhood. What parents can do is to aid in providing a sense of security in personal relationships; this can be a true antidote to a fear of death.

However, the loneliness and fear which children encounter in contemplating death is focused and intensified when death becomes a real actuality for them, either in terms of their own dying or a family member's death. Clearly the most difficult thing dying children must cope with is a sense of alienation that overcomes them as they realize they will be separated forever from their parents. Parents unfortunately contribute to this feeling of alienation by developing a type of self-protection and perhaps unconsciously surrendering the child before he/she dies. Ways in which the parent may do this is by giving away the child's clothes, toys, and other possessions.

Rose Zelige (1974) describes the child's feelings in this way: "The seriously ill child senses that his family is withdrawing from him emotionally as well as physically. He tends to withdraw from his social environment and concentrates on his own illness and fears. As he becomes more and more isolated, he feels alone, unwanted, forgotten, and abandoned. When death seems imminent he, too, begins to separate himself from his family, and direct his attention to his loneliness and his dying" (pp. 3-5).

A basic question then is what can parents, therapists, etc., do to counteract the loneliness experienced by children who are confronted with mortality's meaning, and how can we help to illuminate their basic situation and make more comfortable their transition from confusion to understanding. While there are many possible things to do—like discussing death honestly with children and perhaps taking them to a funeral—one very important thing to do to help children as they begin to recognize the presence and meaning of death is to give them the advantage of a healthy religious faith. There certainly appears to be a very definite correlation between children's religious faith and their ability to accept a realistic view of death. Just the very conception of a caring Deity can be extremely comforting for the disturbed and lonely child.

Finally, the children can be aided simply by caring for them. As Elisabeth Kubler-Ross (1975), who is renowned for her work with the dying, said when she was asked what could possibly counter the terrible discovery of death in a child's life, the most helpful thing in the world is "one person who really cares" (p. 145).

Divorce As a Cause of Loneliness in Children

Another important topic to consider in discussing feelings of loneliness in children is that of *divorce*, especially since the child's sense of self-worth might be affected. Children, for example, might believe they are being abandoned by the parent who leaves because they, the children, are not "good enough." Or the children may simply believe that the divorce is really their fault. This latter feeling may be especially evident in cases where prior to the divorce the spouses argued bitterly about parental responsibilities. Finally, children may simply miss the companionship of the parent who does not have custody. And in cases where both parents have joint custody and the child spends a portion of the year with each parent, disruption may occur in the child's peer and adult relationships as the child moves from one household to another.

Children often simply fear being left alone by their parents, and divorce may make their fears more concrete. Therefore, children need constant reassurance that they won't be abandoned if a divorce were to occur. Richard Gardner (1977) describes the stages of grief a child goes through after he loses one parent through divorce. He compares this grief with the feelings a child experiences after he loses a parent through death, although the stages are not as severe. In the beginning the child may try to deny that the parent is leaving; after this stage, when the parent has actually left, the child may grieve for the now missing parent and be preoccupied with thoughts of this person (p. 101). The final stage in dealing with this loss may be sadness and depression.

When the child experiences these feelings, his/her ability to play and to form peer relationships may well be affected. Of course, time may be the best cure for these feelings, as well as the remaining parent's ability to encourage the child to talk, cry, and release whatever feelings exist. Also, there are renowned organizations like Parents Without Partners and Big Brothers and Sisters of America who may aid in providing emotional support for the child if the parent is too preoccupied with her/her own feelings of pain.

Further, a parent who abandons his/her child may create such a stressful situation that the child may conclude, incorrectly of course, that he/she does not deserve a parent's love. In order to correct this difficult situation, the other parent or guardian should inculcate the belief that the child is worthy of life and that it is a problem with the parent, not a problem or fault in the child, that caused the abandonment.

Obviously, children who are abandoned by a parent or who experience a bitter divorce struggle are much more likely to be distrustful of the stability of other adult and peer relationships. Consequently, they might stay within themselves and refrain from involvements that could provide a substitute love. A living experience which demonstrates love and reliability is therefore the best way to lessen the child's distrust. Even if the absent parent is unable to visit the child, it is always much better if this parent can maintain some type of involvement with the child and assure the child of particular love and interest.

Loneliness and Deprived Children

Deprived children are those who are unfortunate enough to grow up in an "understimulating" environment. This usually occurs in families of low socio-economic status, but also it may possibly occur in homes where the principal parent is depressed and simply unresponsive to his/her child's needs, regardless of economic status. A child who grows up in an emotionally deprived environment may be emotionally unresponsive, listless, and overly quiet. Deprivation may impair development and intellectual growth and may result in cultural and linguistic disadvantages and also may result in an unfavorable total environment, including such factors as poor housing, low income, poorer physical care, unstable family structure, and a culturally impoverished home.

Children who are unfortunate enough to grow up under such conditions frequently have low self-esteem and difficulty in establishing peer and adult relationships and also are frequently failures in school. Clearly, there is no simple solution for this problem. The Head Start Program was an attempt to compensate for the environmental deficiencies of some children, but just a few hours a day cannot completely change the dynamics for children who must deal with such problems each day of their lives.

Abused Children

Child abuse is a very topical item today, as recent magazine articles testify. Indeed, the actual figures or numbers of children suffering from abuse and neglect are probably much greater than percentages reported since many cases go unreported. Physical abuse is simply the most extreme range of parental hostility which has a particularly devastating effect on the child's later development. Physically abused infants and children often demonstrate the "frozen watchfulness" syndrome as they lie motionless, eyes alert, but otherwise wholly expressionless.

Also, children who are victims of abuse often incorporate their parents' negative view of themselves; they view themselves as "bad" and are frequently unable to relate to adults and peers and have difficulties in later life in establishing trustful relationships. The physical effects of child abuse are clearly appalling, but while the physical damage can heal in most cases the psychological damage is more prone to leave lasting scars. Children who are victims of psychological or mental abuse are especially likely to have deep feelings of emptiness and loneliness and a yearning to be cared for; these are the children who may be excessively dependent in later life.

Also, abusive parents tend to be quite critical and expect simply too much from their children. Brandt Steele (1976) has written that abused children are "left with a sense of failure, low self-esteem, and a beginning tendency to believe in the use of physical attack to solve problems . . . the emotional abuse and lack of empathetic understanding are probably more important in causing later character difficulties than the actual pain" (p. 225).

Children who are abused often repeat the pattern and become abusers when they too become parents; indeed, histories of child abuse can be traced through several generations. Parents who were abused as children were often deprived of basic mothering; such parents possessed little self-esteem to sustain them through the stressful periods which any parent encounters.

Children must clearly be removed, in the most extreme cases, from any environment where they are consistently abused. However, this may lower further the children's self-esteem, since they may feel that they are "to blame" for all that has occurred. Children who are victims of child abuse may frequently need intensive therapy to overcome the psychological problems which may result from their extreme rejection. The psychological havoc which abuse brings to a child is great, but worse results can occur: Each year children die, the victims of such violence.

Children Who Feel Set Apart and Different

Minority Children
Around the age of five, children are aware of the societal valuations placed on different sexes and races. Minor-

ity children face special problems; belonging to a minority group is not itself stressful, but in our society where complex prejudices are prevalent, minority children frequently are victims of hurtful attitudes. These children may often feel rejected and angry and may experience feelings of self-belittlement.

Thus minority children in areas where prejudice is rampant and where they are surrounded by the majority often feel a unique type of loneliness and alienation. Such children retreat, not only within their own racial group but also within themselves. Parents of all races owe it to their children to aid them in developing strong and positive feelings about all people regardless of skin, color, sex, socioeconomic status, or culture. Therefore, parents should be sensitive to the development of children's awareness of racial differences and provide factual and logical answers to children's questions about race.

As Phyllis Harrison-Ross and Barbara Wyden (1973) have written: "If a black child is to grow up in this society with a high self-esteem, he has to work harder at it than a white child. . . . Acquaint children with the facts of blackness so they can be strong enough to fulfill their potential" (p. 34). Children, of course, are quite resilient; so, if they are nurtured with love and self-respect by the actions of caring adults, they often discover a path through the maze of alienation and prejudice that may confront the minority child and lead him down a path of loneliness.

Disabled Children
Let us now consider disabled children in more detail than earlier in this chapter. Disabled children also have obvious special problems in their interactions with peers and adults. Many children, as well as adults, have never had to deal with their feelings about the disabled; hence

their responses may range from inappropriate curiosity to derisive or cruel behavior. Parents may become either too *indulgent* with the child or too *punitive* when their disabled child fails to meet their own expectations.

As with the minority child, the most crucial problem for a disabled child is the development of a positive self-concept. Since our culture's reward system values achievement instead of effort, the disabled child, incapable of great or substantial achievement, may not receive a positive feedback for his/her efforts. Therefore, it is vitally important for parents and teachers to value disabled children for their intrinsic worth and their effort if these children are to feel good and possibly a bit more secure about themselves.

However, adults and peers frequently have much difficulty in providing spontaneous feedback for handicapped children because of their own awkwardness around those who are physically different from themselves. The result may very well be tense and fewer social relationships for the disabled child. As Mia Killmer Pringle (1975) has written, "How well a handicapped child makes out in the long run depends far less on the nature, severity, or onset of his condition than on the attitudes of his parents first and foremost, then on those of his peers and teachers, and eventually on society's. . . . These determine how he feels about himself and society" (p. 117).

The disabled child often has particular difficulty establishing meaningful social contact due to difficulties in ambulation, parental overprotection, and peer rejection. Therefore, parents and caring adults must sometimes use creative methods to bring disabled children and their peers together. Also parents can frankly discuss the disability with their child and explain the social stigmas they will encounter. This will help the child to learn effective social skills for dealing with the stigma, from society's viewpoint, of being disabled. As in interracial situations much of the responsibility rests on those who are not in the minority. Parents need to discuss physical differences between people with their children and describe the devastating effects of prejudice in order that children can grow into caring, sensitive adults.

Imaginary Playmates

Many children, especially between ages three and ten, invent imaginary playmates for themselves. However, some parents are worried that such companions that a child conjures up for himself/herself indicate a personality disturbance in their child. While this is rarely the case, psychologists estimate that as many as 15-30 percent of all children have imaginary companions.

As. A. E. Jersild (1965) points out, children probably invent such vivid fantasies out of their creativity, desire for companionship, and need to develop an "ideal interaction with powers, virtues, and privileges" (p. 341) that the child lacks in real life. Most children do abandon such imaginary companions when they enter school and begin to form strong peer relationships. However, when children fail to make their own *real* friends or appear to have difficulties in relating to their peers and/or parents and retreat into a shell of loneliness, adults should certainly worry about their children's imaginary playmates.

Anxiety and the Child

Adults certainly are cognizant of what it is like to feel *anxious*—that gnawing, pervasive feeling of disease which haunts us, often in a more disquieting way because of its lack of specific cause than specific fears or worries which we rationally, on some level at least, deal with. However, anxiety is ordinarily based on specific feelings and fears, such as fear of abandonment, rejection, or failure, or feelings of *loneliness,* which we can easily discover if we probe deeply enough. Adults familiar with anxiety, it seems, often forget that children also share these feelings, even when they cannot verbalize them. Children clearly fear, among many other things, solitude, abandonment, death, and loneliness. Since children may be left for varying reasons and at various times by their primary caretakers, they may well experience abandonment and must deal with the feelings it unleashes; however, the children frequently reconcile these feelings when the parent returns.

Those children who have particular problems with anxiety are those who have been brought up with within the throes of a repressive religious environment. These children are threatened frequently by "fire and brimstone" corrections. Hell is equated with being banished to perpetual darkness, and this becomes a symbol for their unworthiness. Thus these children believe that death is their certain and just reward. Children who have such feelings cannot really develop positive feelings about themselves; the result is that the world often appears to be a dark, hostile, and threatening place. Concomitant with such feelings for children is a fear of the dark, and since many children are left alone to sleep in dark rooms, they associate darkness with being lonely, lost, or abandoned. Parents simply must be more sensitive to their children's fears in these areas.

Anything which lowers children's confidence in themselves only increases their susceptibility to fear and anxiety. As Karen Horney (1945) has so well described, children may attempt to deal with anxiety and the world in three basic ways: 1) by moving *toward* people to achieve feelings of belonging and support; 2) by moving *against* people to fight against hostility; or 3) by moving *away* from people.

Such children simply build worlds of their own—with nature, with dreams.

These latter basic coping patterns are most important. If children learn to deal or cope with the reality of their environment by moving *against* or *away* from people, there is obviously very little chance that they will be able to form satisfactory relationships with those whom they care about (or in the worst cases they will be unable to care about others). These children face lives of loneliness and rejection, with very little love for themselves or from other sources. However, there are clear alternatives to such gloomy circumstances which we shall discuss in this chapter's last section.

Solutions

As should be quite obvious from this chapter, children who are lonely, abandoned, or abused need special assistance. This is not simply an area of concern for mothers, or for child-care specialists like day-care workers and teachers. It is more than a problem for such individuals and experts who make their livelihoods from telling mothers what to do.

How can we hope to recreate the positive aspects of our past and initiate the building of effective human networks, so important in providing companionship, belonging, security, purpose, and support for our children. Jessie Bernard (1974), the anthropologist, has come up with five possible alternatives for child responsibility, ranging from a revolutionary approach of entirely relieving mothers of the responsibility for child care and child rearing to a more conservative approach of providing a wider array of services—for example, medical, educational, and psychological help. Her other suggestions include fathers and relatives providing support and less specializing of mothers in child care, and less isolation of the mother. All of these alternatives need to be mutually exclusive.

It appears too that we need a network of "carers" for children which would include both adults and children of many ages. All people can benefit and grow from such interaction, and "carers" can include foster and biological mothers, fathers, sisters, brothers, aunts, uncles, nurses, and teachers. Once these carers have made a commitment to the child, what specifically can they do to enable the child to overcome any feelings of *isolation* and *loneliness?*

Clearly, these carers can help children to gain sufficient self-confidence in order that they will make an effort to become members of the "network," rather than resigning themselves to an isolated role. Carers can also stimulate discussion among children, whether in school, in churches, or in other community groups concerned with the special problems of friendliness, unpopular, "isolated" peers. In addition, carers can engineer social situations which facilitate social interactions. Perhaps the most useful role carers can play, however, is to aid children in loving and appreciating themselves.

From such personal strengths, feelings of loneliness may well be a source for creative individual growth instead of overwhelming, negative experiences.

References

Bernard, J. *The future of motherhood.* New York: Penguin Books, 1974.

Bettelheim, B. *The uses of enchantment: The meaning and importance of fairy tales.* Pan Books, 1975.

Bowlby, J. *Attachment and loss, Vol. II: Separation.* New York: Basic Books, 1973.

Gardner, R. A. *The parents book about divorce.* Garden City, N.Y.: Doubleday, 1977.

Harrison-Ross, P. & Wyden, B. *The black child: A parent's guide to raising happy and healthy children.* New York: Berkeley Medallion Books, 1973.

Herbert, M. *Problems of children.* London: Pan Books, 1975.

Horney, K. *Our inner conflicts.* New York: Norton, 1945.

Jersild, A. E. *Child psychology,* 5th ed. Englewood Cliffs, N.J.: Prentice-Hall, 1965.

Killinger, J. *The loneliness of children.* New York: Vanguard Press, 1980.

Kubler-Ross, E. *Death: The final stage of growth.* Englewood Cliffs, N.J.: Prentice-Hall, 1975.

Nagy, M. H. The child's view of death. In H. Feifel (Ed.), *The meaning of death,* New York: Graro Hill, 1959.

Packard, V. *A nation of strangers.* New York: David McKay, 1972.

Pringle, M. A. *The needs of children.* New York: Schocken Books, 1975.

Rank, O. *The trauma of birth.* New York: Harper & Row, 1973.

Steele, B. Violence within the family. In R. E. Helfer and C. H. Kempe (Eds.), *Child abuse and neglect: The family and the community.* Cambridge, Mass.: Ballinger Publishing Co., 1976.

Toffler, A. *Future Shock.* New York: Bantam Books, 1971.

Zeligs, R. *Children's experience with death.* Springfield, Ill.: Charles C. Thomas, 1974.

Chapter 4

Loneliness and the Adolescent

Just now I realized something; the trouble with me is that for a long time I have been just an "I" person. All other people say "we." . . . All people belong to a "we" except me (Lauder, 1978; p. 14).

The sad eyes of the aging, the questioning glance of the middle-aged, the doubting look of the adolescent, and the wondering stare of the young child all probe the same central mystery of human consciousness: Who am I? Where do I fit? Whom can I trust? This search is characteristic of human living and is nowhere more obvious than in the emotional and social limbo faced during adolescence. Rarely in the life cycle will the individual be assailed by so many options; never again will so many probing choices and commitments have to be explored: The self must congeal into a reasonably workable identity, for the social world will intrude definitively into the once safely protected—and theoretically limitless—possibilities of infancy and early childhood. The trusted figures of childhood as well as the evolving self will be perceived more critically as fallible and limited. The confirmation of individuality must be achieved.

This confirmation of individuality (individuation) involves many complex changes whereby persons become

71

aware that they are different from other human beings in profoundly significant ways. They will learn that there is a uniqueness in their experience and perceptions which is radically personal, special, and compelling. They will experience the tension between their own interiority and social demands. They will strive to balance the unique sense of self (I) with the interpersonal world (we). It is this continued balancing of varied experiences, needs, hopes, and wants which characterizes the personality and heightens our awareness of the limits of the human condition. Against the background of this awareness the experience of loneliness stands out in bold relief—the experience is ubiquitous, although it evades exact cognitive descriptions. Its definition must be sought in more feeling terms: the disquieting feeling that comes upon us when we are not completely understood—when we experience our radical separateness from all others even in moments of intimacy. It is an ache for meaning. Augustine wrote:

> Everyone is a stranger in this life, in which you see that we are girt round with flesh, through which flesh the heart cannot be seen. . . . In the sojourning of this carnal life each one carrieth their own heart, and every heart is closed to every other heart (Mannin, 1966; p. 52).

Loneliness is experienced in a special developmental way during each stage of the life cycle as the individual struggles to avoid a sense of disenfranchisement and separateness.

> These are the things that stay with us: death, longing, and loneliness and the worst of these is loneliness (Kennedy, 1973; p. 50).

Three parameters must be addressed in considering the experience of loneliness for the adolescent: 1) developmental, 2) cultural, and 3) social. Each of these areas demands highly specific skills which adolescents are in the *process* of acquiring. If they do not acquire them they may find that they are

> on the outside looking in, that nobody seems to need or want him, nobody cares whether he is there or not, that there is no niche for him to fill, no place for him (Kennedy, 1973; p. 38).

One of the major aspects of adolescent loneliness arises from biological individuation and maturation. Physical changes occur in adolescence, heightening the sense of separateness. They impel adolescents into new realms of experience and introduce them into a strange world of needs, wants, hopes, and frustrations. The biology of their experiences is tied directly to their social experiences and growing sense of self. The upsurge of sexual energies, subliminally as well as overtly encouraged by our culture, force adolescents into new and risk-filled searches to find outlets for their energies.

This is also the time when the gender specific differences are encouraged. This involves the adolescents in trying to decipher what is desirable, needed, and appropriate for themselves. It is obvious that the resolution of sexual identity emerges (or should emerge) at this time and the adolescents experience their radical sense of isolation and aloneness as each one struggles to establish what exactly it is "to be an adult." It is the first of many experiences adolescents have which teach them that the data of their own experience based on *their own* bodies may not necessarily be acceptable to other people. For example, adolescents with homo-affective feelings and experiences must encounter the reality that their own needs are held in tension with the society of which they are a (disenfranchised) part. In short, society intrudes to "inform" adolescents just what is and is not appropriate for their body and needs. Since this social demand may not reflect the personal experience of the teenager, there is a heightened sense of aloneness, isolation, and loneliness. As a result involvements become often overwhelmingly difficult for the adolescent who is experiencing a strong revival of sexual drives of all kinds.

These biological changes are inevitable and impel the adolescent into an entirely new personal and social world. They impose upon the adolescent a new sense of burdened isolation:

> The most terrifying burden of the creature is to be isolated, which is what happens in individuation: one separates himself out of the herd. This move exposes the person to the sense of being completely crushed and annihilated because he sticks out so much, has to carry so much in himself. These are the risks when the person begins to fashion consciously and critically . . . [a] framework . . . of self reference (Becker; p. 171).

The loneliness and sense of inadequacy, which are so prevalent in adolescence because of the rapidly changing physical and emotional configurations, manifest themselves in the adolescent's sense of self and society. The various physical changes in adolescence also usher a new physical appearance—and a new series of expectations. No longer are the adolescents able to excuse themselves and their actions with obsolete childhood excuses. No longer will others so happily do things for them that they can do themselves. No longer are they able to be the child that they have been.

Adolescents find themselves confronting—and being confronted by—the fundamental question of self-esteem: "Who am I?" Obviously *some* of the answers to this question will be found in interaction with other people, but a growing sense of self-esteem will necessarily emerge from interaction with a whole new set of worries and responsibilities which also attend adolescence: cars, school, work, drugs, sex, alcohol. These new experiences are most directly linked and reflect a close biological/psychological unity, particularly in the establishment of self-esteem.

Self-esteem, that is, the adolescents' appreciation and acceptance of their self-perception, is critical for successful development of a positive self-concept. As Strommen (1974) points out, perceptions of self influence other relational activities, interests and abilities. When feelings of self-criticism, lack of self-confidence, and low self-worth pummel, they leave their mark on physical well-being *and* effective functioning (p. 14). Often this will involve skin disorders, physical ailments, or debilitating states: linked are also drug abuse, alcoholism, suicide, and other self-defeating behaviors. The establishment of a self-concept which is positive (self-esteem) is the direct result of experiences. This self includes the ideas and feelings about one's body and the qualities of the person's intellectual and personal characteristics. It also involves one's background, values, and beliefs. In childhood, the family is the primary matrix of human relationships and provides the core experience for the development of a positive self-concept. This process is enhanced and accentuated as the child becomes increasingly involved in a wider horizon of human relations in school and play. In adolescence, the forging of a self-identity which is adequate and positive becomes the central task of development. To accomplish this task, the adolescent must turn both to himself and to others. Needless to say, these turnings are accompanied by significant affect, anxiety and tension. The inward journey—reflected in a person's peers—begins to answer the inevitable questions "Who am I? How good am I? Am I lovable?" All of these questions are ways of approaching the question of identity and individuation. The answer to the question "Who" is essentially existential and interpersonal in nature; the response to "How" is essentially social and psychological; the question of lovability is social/personal and spiritual.

While a developing self-concept is linked to bodily changes in adolescence, there are many other elements of significance since the self is as much symbolic as it is physical and social.

Background, biology, property, peers, etc., are all part of "self." The literal "projecting" or "throwing out" of self into the environment underscores a sense of individuation and separation since it seems that, quite literally, the human "exists" in quite separate—and separated—elements like family, property, peers.

The inevitable result of this throwing of self into objects makes the acceptance of the multiple aspects of self more difficult.

> There is very little of such self-acceptance in our society. Much more in evidence are guilt feelings which have little or no connection with any moral faults, and a free-floating anxiety; these drive many people to misery and unhappiness if not to an incapacitating neurosis. Such feelings of guilt and anxiety are almost epidemic in our culture and constitute sure signs of massive self-hate (Greeley, 1961; p. 145).

It is important to note here that self-acceptance does not annul the uneasy feelings of loneliness. In Strommen's study (1974), it was pointed out that most lonely youths can designate some close friends. Apparently loneliness is not cured by company, nor does solitude necessarily increase it. Aloneness is more than physical separation in living. It is akin to the fear of nonbeing or meaninglessness so often identified with the alienation of the twentieth century (p. 20).

The sense of social isolation and physical separateness resulting from biological individuation highlight the discrepancies in the shifting and uncertain self-esteem of the adolescent. In fact, by their very nature, the new physiological changes as well as the concomitant social shifts necessitate exploration on the part of the adolescent. Any exploration obviously leaves much room for experimentation—which sometimes fails. In the rapidly shifting emotional life of the adolescent, failures and losses are rarely construed as "losing" something. Rather, they tend to be internalized in the self-concept as "loser."

Failure and uncertainty seem to heighten feelings of loneliness, and the lonely child is often characterized by repeated failure patterns which confirm their poor self-concept.

> The individual, already a poor performer, begins to regard himself as a loser, becomes anxious, fails even more grandly, thus corroborating—and lowering still more—his rapidly dwindling self-esteem (Siegel & Siegel, 1977; p. 62).

It is as though the lonely adolescent experiences himself as the hopeless object of external forces—the focus of control is completely external. Everything is attributed to people, events, groups outside the person.

Adolescents' experience of alienation based on biological and social changes often leave them with nowhere to turn but to rebellion and escape. Such adolescents confront a double bind: Since they are unable to open their lives to others in caring, committed, and loving ways (an inability which is transient and developmental in nature and results from the interplay of personal versus social experience), they do not experience the type of love and affection which others could give them in return. The very probing quality of their commitments necessitates an incomplete and unpredictable quality to their experience. In some fundamental ways, the love one *gives and receives* is the foundation stone for self-esteem and self-worth. Since adolescents are developmentally precluded from completely understanding and responding to these situations, they are trapped in a double bind. In loneliness, fear, and impaired self-esteem, they try to search the meaning of life. Causes and effect intertwine, loneliness begetting low self-esteem and low self-esteem begetting loneliness.

The loss of identity is the ultimate cause of our Age of Apathy. Young Americans are apathetic because they feel that they are anxious, because they feel the threat of meaninglessness, and they should be anxious because meaninglessness has infiltrated into the core of their personalities. They have no strong communities to which to give their allegiances, no visionary ideals to struggle for, no realistic self-image to try to sustain and develop, no symbols to explain the world around them, and no personality core to orient them as they drift into a disorganized society. They are forced to move into the problems of adulthood much as a tiny cork floats down a rapidly moving river toward a stormy sea. They would like to rebel yet feel that they have as much chance to change things as the cork does the ocean. Unfortunately, they are often right (Gordon, 1976; p. 85).

Cultural Sources of Loneliness

This problem of the confusion between the cause and effect of loneliness is, in part, due to the complex relationship between adolescence and society. This inability of adolescents to relate to our society is more obvious than it may at first seem. While the adolescents are searching for highly personalized and significant selves, the culture demands from them conformity—or at least uncomfortable interdependence on a technological world, one which is metallic and depersonalized. As adults we are so accustomed to the technological world that we discount its effects on the more supple personalities of the adolescent:

> Thus, though barraged with discussions of our rapidly changing world, and "recent developments," we too easily can remain incognizant of the enormous significance, and in many ways the historical uniqueness, of social change in our society. . . . Rapid changes in all aspects of life mean that technologies, all institutions, and all values are open to revisions and obsolescence.

> Continual innovation as we experience it in this country profoundly affects our conception of ourselves, our visions of the future, the quality of our attachment to the present, and the myths we construct of the past. It constitutes one of the deepest sources of strain in American life, and many characteristically "American" outlooks, values, and institutions can be interpreted as attempts to adapt to the stress of continual change (Kenniston, 1961; p. 88).

The increase in rapid scientific and technologic changes often deprives younger people of the sense of belonging. This is intensified by the necessary increase in mobility. We feel sharply cut off from primary groups and from extended family ties. We no longer participate *directly* in the creation production of needs for either ourself or our family. Such a self-sufficient economy has been replaced by the assembly line. Ironically, adolescents experience themselves as more and more disenfranchised and lonely, while at the same time they are viewed as increasingly designated "valuable" by the larger society of which they are a part.

But their value resides in what they can do in terms of concrete technologic contribution not in terms of *who they are:*

> The individual fulfills his role in order to attain a higher reward, not because there is intrinsic value in being one's self, but because there is an economic value toward which one is directed. With advances in production, with the development of mechanical and automotive devices, with the change from rural to urban living, with the emphasis on making other's services indispensable, man has become increasingly competitive, exploitative, status conscious, and suspicious of his neighbor. . . . Modern man lives without a personal world in which he has meaningful and enduring ties (Moustakus, 1975; p. 210).

The continuing depersonalization and the consequent realization of the uncertainty and unpredictability of the future provides for an inordinate emphasis on the *present* and surviving "self." One tends to discount what has gone before and looks to the future uncertainly.

> Industrial-urban society of the twentieth century has a number of characteristics that seem to be conducive to loneliness (Bowna, 1955; p. 141).

What other vision could the adolescent develop except to pessimistically

> look upon the adult world as a cold, mechanical, abstract, specialized, and emotionally meaningless place in which one simply goes through the motions (Kenniston, 1961; p. 62).

It is naive to assume that technology will abate in favor of more humanistic motivations, and one must look squarely at what is happening. There is an increased sense of powerlessness, disenfranchisement, separation of generations, and technological control.

It is a frightening enough feeling for a teenager to realize that he or she cannot hold his or her act together. But in the past that feeling was mediated by the sense that the adult world offered the possibility of security. Growing up today, kids not only feel that their parents are too involved in their own changes to bother with their problems, they also feel that the adult world offers them no models they would like to imitate, that being an adult means only more of the same . . . more insecurity, more instability, more unhappiness (Gordon, 1976; p. 59).

These changes are really inextricably united since the technological age also offers chances for advancement, and this requires continued mobility. The mobility in today's world is another factor in the adolescents' loneliness. It is a particular type of loneliness since it reflects a series of relationships which have either been broken or never made. As adolescents undergo the distinctly developmental task of becoming less dependent on their parents and as they begin to reach out, they experience the continued mobility and cultural atmosphere as underscoring their sense of loss and aloneness. Frequently the relinquishing of parental attachment is completed only to learn that there are no immediate subsequent relationships with other people immediately available. It is the loneliness, not of loss, but of a desire for intimacy.

Talking to groups of young people in the cities and suburbs around the nation, one is struck by the effect of mobility on the formation of friendships and larger peer groups. Families move so often that children have little chance to form stable relationships with those of their own age (Gordon, 1976; p. 85).

The increased mobility, technological emphasis, and de-creasing family size also tend to limit the individual's chances for reaching out to others. The extended family which once provided an entire range of cultural support has become scarce in middle-class America and has been replaced by the nuclear family. The nuclear family is par-ticularly subject to mobility and this mobility itself is one of the major factors in contributing to adolescent loneliness.

> This loss is still greater when the larger kinship group is con-sidered, for modern mobility separates relatives and lessens communication. The kinship solidarity of a rural society where relatives live near each other and work together is under-mined by the movement of people from place to place. In many families today relatives see each other only during spe-cial occasions such as holidays, weddings, or funerals (Bowna, 1955; p. 95).

The problem is considerably deeper than loneliness based on rootlessness or inability to meet new people to replace the family ties. The loneliness of adolescence is a very specific kind of experience which arises from the ado-lescent's personal development as well as social demands. The loneliness of adolescence is based on a profound awareness of difference and separateness from all others—even their families as well as a sense of alienation within their own families. The alienation is based on a lack of trust of the family and a confusion about the family's ability to support them. The mistrust, it seems, is directly related to loneliness—and well-founded in the adolescent's experi-ence.

> Even before the adolescent gets out of school he may begin to perceive that the standards and practices in social classes to which he aspires are different from those in his own back-

ground. As a result of this observation the manners, morals, and precepts of the family may be looked upon with growing condescension or mistrust (Bowna, 1955; p. 95).

The adolescent's involvement with his or her family at this stage in development provides a double-bind: As the adolescent moves toward adulthood there is a need to reach out to peers and to establish emotional attachments. An already difficult developmental task is compounded by the increased mobility and simultaneous isolation going on within the nuclear family today. The increased period of economic dependence necessary for the adolescent within today's culture may also hinder adolescents as they attempt to move beyond their families. Somehow this dilemma must be negotiated.

In adolescence social participation becomes even more critical to development: The group of friends makes possible expression of the unique concerns of the adolescent and permits each adolescent to feel that no matter how different his or her feelings and outlook are from those of his or her parents, they are valid. Distress at social isolation, at being "left out" appears very early and is increasingly painful. The latency child without others with whom to play may only wistfully watch from the sidelines or morosely complain to adults, but as the child becomes older and enters adolescence, the issue of acceptance attains almost overwhelming importance (Weiss, 1973; p. 57).

Luckily, on some fronts the adolescent's experience also expands in a positive direction, and the entrance into high school provides a new arena for the exploration of experiences and people. But as their new world of peers opens, some adolescents become lost and lonely as their childhood friends regroup themselves and explore new behaviors.

In addition, they also find a sense of powerlessness and meaninglessness in the schools, the one institution within our society
where one would hope human values would prevail above
all. . . . It is Friedenberg's contention that the school, if it
does not create it, certainly reinforces the tension that is found
in our society between originality, innovation, and individual
excellence and the necessity of fitting into the general pattern
of mass culture (Fitzpatrick, 1976; p. 148).

Often these new groupings and rituals of entrance are
based on criteria which the adult world itself generates
through the granting or withholding of approval such as
academic achievement and athletics. When students are
classified according to such arbitrary standards, without
recognition of the diversity of individual skills, a game is
set with severe competition, which for many produces a
sense of losing, failing, and being lonely.

The growing tendency of using test scores to classify students
and schools contributes to student separation and is a perver-
sion of the original purpose of learning assessment. When
students are continuously measured against a norm based on
questionable standards and are found wanting, they experience a feeling of failure and its attendant loneliness. Assessment for the purpose of diagnosing important learning needs
is helpful only when the testing information is used to help
students move successfully through school according to their
individual learning rates and styles (Robert, 1973; p. 96).

There is, of course, the flip side of the coin where the
adolescents may be set apart because of "success"—the
class "brain." This is especially true if they do not have
other interests and talents in such areas as athletics, music,
or drama.

It seems that the adolescent must always negotiate the

delicate interrelationship between freedom, choice, and loneliness. This has been, perhaps, most adequately expressed in the 1974 Yale College welcoming speech by Kingman Brewster:

> Welcome to the burdens which this largely permissive university imposes upon you. . . . To be offered so much choice leaves you a little lonely. To have it left up to you is somewhat isolating. . . . These harassments of being on your own . . . will soon pass. But there is a heavier and more longlasting burden which you cannot escape. . . . Yours is the burden of having to find out for yourself what matters most, what you care most about, what you believe, what you most want to do with your life (1974, p. 45).

Over and over again, it becomes clear that loneliness manifests itself in a myriad of ways which interphase developmental, cultural, and social concerns. It is to these social aspects of loneliness that we will now turn our attention. We will try to focus on the corollary issues of uprootedness, alienation, moral confusion, and emerging and alternative lifestyles with this social context as well.

Social Sources of Loneliness

The unit of social life during adolescence is a small group that adolescents often refer to as "the crowd" or "the kids I hang out with," which sociologists and psychologists label as "the peer group." Early adolescents, confronted with new social expectations at puberty, shift their dependency needs from the family to small often unisexual cliques composed of adolescents of approximately the same age. These cliques are, or become, subsystems in crowds, which are in turn composed of all male cliques, all female cliques, and more mature male and female cliques (White & Speisman, 1977; p. 88). This last grouping of peers is typically composed of an equal number of boys and girls. The core of it contains six to eight members, with perhaps another six or so adolescents on the fringes of the group. Those who are steady members of the group usually live within driving distance of one another, attend the same school, and come from basically the same socioeconomic background (Cole & Hall, 1970; p. 347).

Roles of varying importance are ascribed to the adolescent peer group. Psychologists generally agree that the "peer culture" (the sum total of spontaneous social manifestations among age-mates) is an influential force during adolescence, particularly during the middle years of adolescence (Cole & Hall, 1970; p. 347). One of the strongest needs of adolescence is to be supported and approved by peers. Due to this fact, the peer group is a powerful force in setting standards of behavior and attitudes.

Peer group membership offers many positive contributions to the growth toward identity which is intensely experienced during adolescence. Adolescents learn their position in relation to other people and decisions are made about social and moral behavior which have been previously formulated in the home, school, and church. During inevitable periods of alienation from parents and the family, the peer group offers adolescents a forum in which they can communicate with people of their own age. A sense of security is gained in sharing some problems with peers. Adolescents often experience in the peer group the feeling that they are needed, a feeling crucial to a person's self-image throughout all stages of life. One of the greatest gifts that the peer group offers is that of empathy. When one's own peer group admits that they know "just how you feel" the burden of the particular adolescent crisis is lightened. Perhaps most importantly, the peer group reinforces structures of individual characteristics given by parents, and at the same time opens the mind of the adolescent to other moral values and concepts than those which have been instilled by the parents and family (Wagner, 1971; p. 58). Through this simultaneous process of reinforcing and opening up, the peer group provides a social environment in which adolescents decide what kind of persons they will become.

While there are many benefits in peer group membership we must also consider the ways in which peer group pressures contribute to the loneliness of the adolescent.

To do this it is necessary to determine the various ways that the peer group alienates the adolescent and the reasons for this alienating behavior. An additional important consideration is how adult interaction with the peer group also affects this alienation.

Behavior required for peer group acceptance may contradict the adolescent's inner expectations of self. When the need to conform comes into conflict with the need for self-direction, alienation results. Zachry (1974) clarifies this point: Adolescents normally are uneasy about dissimilarities that threaten their security among peers and the solidarity of their group. However, they are also uneasy about the dissimilarities that jeopardize their success in the struggle to be important, to be persons in their own right (p. 162). In this broadest sense, alienation is a common experience for all adolescents in their balancing of the value of belonging with the value of establishing their own identity.

Adolescents expect their friends to provide some reaction to, or reflection of, their "self" that might provide a true likeness or image pattern. This reflection is preferably provided by people who are simultaneously undergoing similar changes, conflicts, and unheavals (Gray & Garer, 1974; p. 302). When individuals desire to be part of a group that fulfills this need, they are said to view the desired group as a reference group. As individuals strive for membership in a reference group, they take on certain attitudes and opinions of the group prior to entering it (Littrell & Eicher, 1973; p. 57). This strong peer group need during adolescence magnifies the impact of peers. Cooperation is stressed with the group with which they identify and strong emphasis is placed on this cooperation even if the goal to which the group aspires is socially defined as negative (Konopka, 1973; p. 306). If the goal is negative, adolescents are often forced to choose between alienation from the reference group for not cooperating in achieving the goal, or alienation from significant others, especially parents, for cooperating in attaining the negative goal. The "damned if you do, damned if you don't" dilemma is an alienating one, and depending upon the strength of the need for membership in the reference group, these adolescents find themselves in bad standing with either friends or parents.

Adolescents may experience alienation due to their peer group associations based on parents' expectations of the adolescent. In the Newmans' study (1976) this aspect of adolescent alienation is explored. To the extent that adolescents' peer associations reflect their parents' values and goals, there will be minimal conflict over friendships, but there still may be considerable pressure for adolescents to take an active part in social activities (p. 267). However, parents may pressure their adolescents into membership in peer groups that do not offer them acceptance. The alienating effects on adolescents placed in such circumstances is obvious. Not only do they not fit in with a particular peer group, but also alienation in the home results due to their failure to live up to the parents' goals.

Zachry (1974) identifies two other common sources of peer group alienation rooted in relationships with parents. If throughout the life of their children parents have dominated or shown little affection for them adolescents tend to suspect that peers do not want them and magnify small acts of neglect on their part into deliberate rudeness, or to imagine slights where none exist. Second, the adolescent is confronted with two sets of values, two moral codes: that of their parents, and that of their peer groups. Adolescents cannot always go the whole way with the gang, however much they may wish to do so. This conflict is essential to further growth toward responsible self-reliance, but it also has the immediate effect of alienation to some degree from the peer group due to lack of conformity to the group's moral code. If the differences between the moral standards of the family and the peer group are significant, this threatens a deeper source of security—deep-seated identification with the family (p. 162).

Peer group expectations may be too distant from adolescents' own values. This results in a persistent experience of tension and conflict as adolescents try to balance the allure of peer group membership with the cost of abandoning personal beliefs. Such conflicts are painful and confusing, and if these tensions become too great, the adolescents may not open up to the group, preventing them from achieving a sense of group identity (Newman & Newman, 1976; p. 270).

Two additional situations resulting in alienation for the adolescent are worth noting. The individual adolescent may not like any peer group, or conversely, no peer group may offer acceptance to the individual. In this outright exclusion from any peer group, either self- or other-imposed, the adolescent experiences a sense of alienation.

If these experiences become the norm for an individual it will be virtually impossible for the person eventually to achieve an integrated ego-identity (Erikson) or group identity (Newman). Fortunately, positive resolution of these alienating situations usually occurs. Horrocks and Benimoff (1971) note that personal acceptability to others at any given time depends upon the role adolescents are perceived as playing, together with a judgment of their adequacy to cope with the demands of the role in the specific situation in which it is being played. Research findings support the claim that it may well be that individuals are sometimes found unacceptable not because of themselves or the situation, but because of the selector's own feelings of inadequacy (p. 42). If adolescents feel that they really aren't qualified to be a member of a particular peer group to which they aspire, often the feelings of inadequacy will be the cause of their alienation from a particular peer group.

Adolescents are faced with a social system which ascribes varying degrees of status to membership in different peer groups. High-school students recognize but don't understand the status system into which they are organized. Low status students try to model themselves after the members of the peer group to which they aspire. In the adolescent's inability to move upward,

> it is difficult to describe the pain the average student suffers as he tries to grapple with a system he does not comprehend and cannot change. The only way he can explain it is that he is deeply flawed. He feels he is really handicapped. fearing that his defect will be discovered and that he will be made to suffer as before, his whole life becomes a cover up. Nothing can release him from a haunting sense of inadequacy, except an understanding of the system that bred it (Jones, 1976; p. 327).

Jones continues emphatically,

> We are victims of a vicious self-inflicted social system. We will carry its effects forever. Some will emerge into society filled with confidence and security while others will emerge assured that they are, and always will be, losers (p. 327).

Adolescents are confronted with three options: They may become a member of the high-status group, they may deal with their alienating experiences by ascribing value to membership in a peer group to which the social system does not, or they may equate recurring experiences of alienation from high-status peer groups as evidence of a "deep flaw" and have to deal with the resulting feelings of loneliness based on a lowered self-image.

Although higher status is attributed to certain peer groups and not others, our social system is designed in such a way that it reinforces the status system, rather than minimize it. One practical suggestion mentioned by Jones is that high school curriculum and activities be designed to incorporate the frequent movement of students into different groupings (p. 327). It is important for the counselor of alienated youth to recognize and understand the social environment, with its ascribed status to particular peer groups. Counselors of alienated youth must place increasing importance on their preventative role, as opposed to the more traditional treatment.

It is also important to realize the crucial role the peer group plays in alleviating the loneliness of the adolescent. Peer groups may be the main outlet and support for adolescents when they experience alienation from other significant people in their lives. These associations can provide a feeling of being needed, central to the development of a positive self-image. Peer group membership for the adolescent contains the tension of being both a primary source of alienation, as well as a primary basis for handling feelings of loneliness. At best the adolescent is able to recognize and respond to the peer group within this dialectical framework.

Adolescents, in their exposure to experiences of loneliness through peer group relationships, have the opportunity to become more insightful regarding self, others, and reality. As Lauder (1978) remarks, "the feeling of loneliness suggests that life ought not to be like this, that a person ought not to be totally alone. What loneliness can reveal to us is our most radical need, our deepest drive, our most important desire. Loneliness tells us that to be a person we must love and be loved" (p. 45). Adolescents then, need to recognize periods of loneliness for what they are, as possible opportunities for clarification and integration of personal identity.

Religious/Ethical Education of the Lonely Adolescents

Briefly, it is important to note some implications for educating the alienated adolescent, based on the insights into how peer groups cause this alienation and the accompanying feelings of loneliness. Youth alienation is the "collapse of self-regulatory and self-predictive skills in terms of future oriented behavior and action" (Schiamberg, 1973; p. 98). Importantly, Schiamberg notes that this definition broadens the counseling beyond the traditional process of talk, empathy, sharing of feelings, and mutual understanding. This process needs to be reexamined and focused in terms of action and behavior in a total environment and the design of a total action system. Such a "systems approach to counseling alienated youth" requires broad community-based programs to solve problems such as youth alienation which are manifested in individual personalities but have their roots in the organization of the total social system.

Counselors and educators must consider the "preventive" role that their understanding of the social system can serve. Counseling and religious education of the alienated adolescent has traditionally centered on treatment of symptoms, such as feelings of lack of self-worth and loneliness, but it must also concentrate on preventing the development of social systems which promote alienating experiences.

In this preventive sense Schiamberg notes that along with the counselors' and educators' traditional role of improving individuals' self-understanding, they must assume the role of ombudsman. As ombudsman, the counselor and educator acts as mediator and innovator in improving and exploring the environment of youth.

> The ombudsman-counselor role presupposed a recognition that youth live in a total environment, and that the helping relationship involves helping youth by promoting changes in that environment and helping them to deal with their emotions, feelings, and self-concepts in the more traditional counseling setting (Schiamberg, 1973; p. 98).

In a school setting, the religious educator should be able to make "recommendations to school administrators about proposed changes and improvements in the organization of the school which will facilitate youth development" (p. 123). In relationship to peer group influence on adolescent loneliness, the counselor should achieve an overall understanding of the environment that breeds and reinforces such influence and be in a position to recommend changes that may alleviate alienating influences. It is essential that research continue to establish models for religious educators to use as bases from which to work in optimally organizing a given environment. The aim of this research should be to reduce as much as possible the alienating aspects of adolescent peer groups and the consequential feelings of loneliness which, if intense and consistent enough, as research tells us they are for a significant number of adolescents, can leave scars for life.

In summary, the research review indicates definitive links between peer-group relationships and loneliness in the life of the adolescent. Directions for future research in this area should concentrate on finding practical ways of restructuring existing social systems to minimalize the peer-group influences on loneliness, while maintaining the numerous and necessary advantages of peer-group membership in the adolescent's attempt for an integrated identity.

Conclusion

Loneliness is neither good or bad, moral or immoral. It is human. As Lauder (1978) points out,

> Loneliness can lead to discouragement and even despair and suicide, but it need not. It might lead to insight, to deeper understanding, to more realistic living, to more unselfish loving. We can't always control feelings; we can control the decisions and choices we make because of our feelings. The feeling of loneliness can crush us, but it need not (pp. 22-23).

Adolescents are at a life stage where they are extremely susceptible to feelings of loneliness. They must learn to deal with these feelings, understand their source and their purpose, and creatively use them as means to deeper insight into self and reality. This learning process should be the primary aim of adolescent education and counseling.

References

Becker, E. *The denial of death.* New York: Free Press, 1973.

Brewster, K. So you poor little lambs won't lose your way. *New York Times,* 11 September 1974.

Bowna, C. J. Loneliness and social change. *American Journal of Psychiatry,* 1955, 194, 140-155.

Cole, L. & Hall, I. N., 1955, *Psychology of adolescence.* New York: Holt Rinehart, 1970.

Fitzpatrick, D. J. *The spiritual exercise and religious education.* New York: Alba House, 1976.

Gordon, S. *Lonely in America.* New York: Simon and Schuster, 1976.

Gray, D. & Garer, E. The congruency of adolescent self-perceptions with those of parents and best friends. *Adolescence,* Summer 1974, 302.

Greeley, A. M. *Strangers in the house.* New York: Sheed and Ward, 1961.

Horrocks, J. & Benimoff, M. Isolation from the peer group during adolescence. *Adolescence,* Spring 1971.

Jones, S. High school social status as a historical process. *Adolescence,* Fall 1976.

Kennedy, E. *Living with loneliness.* Chicago: Thomas More Press, 1973.

Kenniston, K. K. Social change and youth in America. In Erik H. Erikson (Ed.), *Youth: Challenge and change.* New York: Basic Books, 1961.

Konopka, G. Requirements for healthy development of adolescent youth. *Adolescence,* Fall 1973.

Lauder, R. *Loneliness is for loving.* Notre Dame, Ind.: Ave Maria Press, 1978.

Littrell, M. and Eicher, J. Clothing opinions and the social acceptance process among adolescents. *Adolescence,* Summer 1973.

Mannin E. E. *Loneliness.* London: Hutchins, 1966.

Moustakas, C. E. *The touch of loneliness.* Englewood Cliffs, N.J.: Prentice-Hall, 1975.

Newman, P. & Newman, B. Early adolescence and its conflict: Group identity vs. alienation. *Adolescence,* Summer 1976.

Robert, M. *Loneliness in the schools.* Niles, Ill.: Argus Communications, 1973.

Schiamberg, L. *Adolescent alienating.* Columbus, Ohio: Charles Merrill, 1973.

Siegel, E. & Siegel, R. *Creating instructional sequences.* Novato, Calif.: Academic Therapy Publication, 1977.

Strommen, M. *Five cries of youth.* New York: Harper & Row, 1974.

Wagner, H. The increasing importance of the peer group during adolescence. *Adolescence,* Spring 1971.

Weiss, R. *Loneliness: The experience of emotional and social isolation.* Cambridge, Mass.: MIT Press, 1973.

White, K. & Speisman, J. *Adolescence.* Monterey, Calif.: Brooks-Cole, 1977.

Zachry, J. *Emotion and conduct in adolescence.* New York: Holt Rinehart, 1974.

Chapter 5

The Mid-Life Journey

Life's journey takes many precarious twists and turns before reaching its destination. Life's journey traverses an obstacle course which can assume the form of stepping stones or stumbling blocks. Any time of change, for most individuals, can be both challenging and confusing; consequently, the individual splits between welcoming and resisting change. Therefore, it is indeed fortunate that life's major changes seldom arrive abruptly but occur over a period of time, their arrival being softened by a continuous transition which acts as a bridge from one critical stage to another.

Specifically, people in mid-life experience change as they progress through childhood, adolescence, and early adulthood, but this barely decreases the later transition's impact, since mid-life brings these individuals to some of life's most drastic changes and puzzling perceptions—one of the most important being a growing recognition of death's inevitability and utter finality.

The mid-life cycle's vastness of change becomes assured simply by its length. For example, one might consider the fact that childhood extends for a period of twelve to fifteen years and is followed by a similar period for adolescence, with early adulthood consisting of just a decade. Mid-life, however, covers a quarter of a century, clearly the longest period in an average lifespan.

While the mid-life transition signifies the journey from youth's waning, with its concomitant ideals, dreams, and aspirations, to old-age's beginning, not everyone makes this transition gracefully. However, each person must react in his/her own way to the verifiable fact that he/she is now considered an adult, one who has reached maturity.

Of course, there is a distinction one must make between being an adult and acting in an adult way. Adulthood, in common usage, may be defined in two ways: as a noun referring to chronological age and as an adjective to describe experiences, institutions, and persons. In addition, one might use adulthood to designate a psychosocial ideal or the attainment of maturity.

Perhaps Maslow's (1964) description of maturity captures best what the mid-life person would be like after a successful passage from early childhood. His person would have a more efficient perception of reality and be comfortable with it and not be threatened by the unknown. This person would also have an acceptance of himself/herself and other people, would be able to experience the new and not be inundated with prejudices. This person would also be objective about solving problems and not lose a sense of self in the problem. In addition, this person would have social feelings of identification, sympathy, and affection, would have a sense of ethical certainty, and exhibit some creativeness (p. 71).

The preceding, of course, gives a description of the ideal, which only a few attain. Certainly, it is a rare individual who approaches mid-life without giving at least a wistful backward glance or does have a twinge of regret regarding unfulfilled youthful dreams and aspirations. A desperate few react to the "mid-life crisis" by reaching back in a attempt to recapture their youth, only to realize later what a futile and destructive gesture this can be.

However, most people in mid-life have made the critical decisions to affect the rest of their lives. But for those who are *approaching* mid-life, their task has shifted. In order for them to attain normalcy as mid-life adults, they must achieve adult and social responsibility, establish and maintain an economic standard of living, develop adult leisure-time activities, etc.

What are mid-life's *positive aspects?* First of all, frequency of illness and disability certainly increase with the years, but the frequency of accidents declines. While most older adults tire more quickly, have higher blood pressure and more dental problems, as well as require more recuperation time from fatigue and illness, they are still less susceptible to colds and allergies. In general, adults get more chronic illnesses but fewer acute illnesses than those younger than they. Maintaining vigor throughout one's adult years is clearly possible, and much deterioration can either be postponed or reversed.

Economically, the mid-life years should be one's best years. During this period people achieve their peak earning level, and as one's children become adults, this usually results in the family's financial affluence, giving parents the opportunity to enjoy this affluence.

Hence, the mid-life years have many positive aspects, but whether these outweigh the negative ones depends greatly on an individual's maturity and how well one has managed one's life and adjusted to change.

However, the potential for loneliness in one's mid-years is great; the time span alone guarantees this. In addition, as age advances, mobility tends to decline, as does the opportunity to mingle with others, consequently narrowing the prospects for communication which many people require to ward off loneliness. Only those possessing deep inner resources can modify being lonely when they spend much time *alone*. In general, however, loneliness in mid-life is associated with specific lifestyles and is, surprisingly, less of a problem than one might expect.

Further, according to research, loneliness doesn't play a major part in mid-life, especially for those who partake of marriage and parenthood. However, at this stage of mid-life, the two sexes diverge radically in their experience of loneliness. Although marriage generally reduces loneliness, the effect is much more marked for men, single men being the most likely and married men the least likely to suffer from loneliness.

Women, however, whether single or married, fall between the two extremes. But up to the early thirties, married women are actually more prone to depression than either single women or married men. According to one survey, 42 percent of British mothers who are confined to their homes with young children to look after suffer from clinical depression.

Men of this age have a different problem if they work in a structured hierarchical profession. They feel that it is dangerous to become overly friendly with colleagues who might become rivals. Also, satisfaction with marriage is lower than at any other stage of the life cycle, as the divorce figures certainly show. Divorce clearly fosters loneliness, and divorcees are more prone to mental and physical illness than married people, leading to a higher suicide rate. However, they seem to recover quite quickly, since half of all divorcees find a new partner within a year, and three quarters remarry within three years.

Mid-life then seems to be one of the least lonely periods of life. Perhaps this age's unique double burden—it's the only time we have responsibility for the generations below and above us—leaves no time to feel lonely. There is little evidence in Britain, for example, of the malaise American psychiatrists term the mid-life crisis. Nor do the majority of us seem to suffer much from the empty nest syndrome—the result of children leaving home. Indeed, surveys suggest that most parents actually look forward to this happening and welcome the chance to spend more time together and to develop new interests.

However, in the present economic climate, a new threat may be looming. The late forties are the beginning of the decade in which redundancy and enforced early retirement are most likely. Both of the latter may involve the loss of friends, although a large American survey discovered no connection between employment status and loneliness among middle-aged women. Despite this problem and the fact that many women become uneasy about reaching the end of their reproductive lives, mid-life is a period when marriages which have survived this far tend to become more rather than less secure.

At this point it seems advisable to discuss some of the psychology regarding mid-life. First of all, the terms "middle age" and "middle life" do not denote precisely *specific* years; instead, these terms refer to a process during the life span's middle section that includes growth and development as well as aging and decline.

Ages forty to sixty or sixty-five have often been considered the middle years, but based on a strictly chronological point of view, ages twenty-four to forty-eight would be life's middle years. Unlike early child development, this period of life is not delineated by any precise physiological phenomena; therefore, the definition of middle age must be approached from psychosocial and psychodynamic perspectives.

Traditionally, stage theories of development connote or

suggest a progressive sequence of qualitative changes in either structure or function, but concepts of stage theory are rather questionable, implying such assumptions as a necessary sequence, universality, and purpose. Middle age, as this chapter has already suggested, is not *uniformly* characterized by illness, widowhood, etc. Stage theory is most useful and most valid in childhood.

Crisis is closely identified with stage theory, and it indicates a decisive turning point, the course of which can be toward improvement or deterioration. A crisis provides possibility for growth as well as for illness.

Clearly, America is middle-age oriented, despite the fact that this country is often described as a youth and child oriented culture. The middle-aged may be looked on as upstarts, incompetents, or whatever by the young, but to the young the middle-aged are *the* Establishment. The center of political and social power resides in the middle, so it is not really surprising that both young and old regard themselves as out-groups and tend to bear common causes.

While no exact, identifiable physical changes typify middle age, general trends do occur. For example, the most distinctive feature is the experiencing of various intimations of mortality, such as development of chronic illnesses, routine medical checkups, etc. Physical changes, even if they are not directly impairing, may create a variety of psychological and emotional reactions, such as fear, anxiety, grief, depression, etc. Certain stress illnesses like stress polycythemia occur commonly.

What about economic aspects or factors? The middle-aged face extraordinary financial burdens, especially middle-aged *workers* who may have serious employment problems. They are unemployed longer than younger people are, secure jobs at less pay, and are admitted less frequently to retraining programs. Also, the middle-aged may burn out in their jobs or become bored with their jobs and find themselves trapped.

Many middle-aged persons also begin to perceive that they have been existing under the dangerous illusion that their Social Security, pensions, etc., will provide them with a secure old age. However, neither existing government programs nor personal providence guarantees security.

With respect to psychological aspects, a number of critical underlying themes in the middle years are apparently present, despite marital and family status, gender, or economic level. Some of these themes are discussed below, and it is generally held that they occur whether or not an external stimulus or crisis is present. However, the means to cope and the kinds of reactions vary.

The first underlying theme is the prime of life, and middle age has been termed the prime of life, a time when the individual attains the height of his power, personal accomplishment, physical maturity, etc. The very image of middle life as life's prime assists in offsetting its negative stereotype of decline. When a middle-aged person's achievement is essentially in accord with his/her promise and ambition, it is a period of quite positive self-confidence, pleasure, and fulfillment which also may signify an affirmative change in direction.

In old age the autobiographical process appears to reveal itself as a life review, but in the middle age it has the quality of stocktaking, the central and most important question being what to do with the rest of one's life. At one extreme, one may shut down all possibilities and thus develop a sense of fatalism; at the other extreme, one might become overexpansive, as revealed in confusion and disorganization.

Another critical issue is fidelity because faithfulness to obligations and observances and loyalty to friends, spouses, and institutions cannot be taken for granted as set for life. Fidelity is an active process which refers to the conscious and unconscious testing of personal and professional commitments. Revisions and quite new commitments may certainly follow, or old commitments may be more firmly established.

Clearly, middle age is the time when one frequently feels overwhelmed by stimuli and too many obligations and duties. Frequently, there is an essential joylessness about the middle years, accompanied by a type of weariness even in success. One may have a feeling of being submerged and engulfed in seemingly insignificant and trivial occurrences, leading perhaps to fatigue.

Similarly, there might be a great desire to streamline one's communications, and one might decide to cultivate only those relationships in which matters are easily understood and communicated. On the negative side of the ledger, however, there are distinct possibilities of repetitiveness, boredom, and impatience.

The middle age of both men and women appears to occur at different times. Women experience middle age earlier than men, usually at a point when they pass beyond the child-bearing age, whether they are childless or not, and when the children, if there are any, leave home. Men in their work careers tend to experience the issue of success or failure somewhat later than women.

Episodes of anxiety and depression are omnipresent in middle age, anxiety being customarily connected with threats to one's personal, physical, and social integrity. When such threats occur, the resulting anxiety may lead to overreaction, possibly hypochondria. On the other hand, depression follows losses, which can occur with numbing frequency in the middle years. Losses, such as anxiety, may be met with excessive reactions, severe depression, etc.

A plethora of disappointments, worries, and increasing pressure can combine to produce serious mental symptoms; indeed, some persons feel that they have missed an opportunity or are not in step with what is deemed normal.

Another frequent and necessary accompaniment of the middle years is *grief*. Only after effective grief-work can any efforts at restitution begin to make another beginning in one's work, to reassess goals, etc.

Certain reactions appear to be common in middle life, reactions like denial, projection, rigidity, etc. However, these means of avoiding a threat or loss are not satisfactorily protective in helping the person to adjust.

Bodily changes are especially noticeable in mid-life, as well as an awareness of such changes like periodontal problems, rheumatic pains, loss of hair, etc. Middle-aged persons may practice denial, may take reasonable steps for routine physical checkups, or may become excessively preoccupied with their own health to the point of hypochondria. Psychosomatic illnesses are common, as is oral dependency.

In mid-life there is a plenitude of problems related to marriage and divorce. People can grow, develop, and change at different rates. For example, one spouse might discover that the other spouse is not quite the same person as when he/she married. Actually, both partners have changed and evolved, but not necessarily in complementary directions. Certain aspects or qualities of marital deterioration and divorce are perhaps related to quite specific aspects of middle life—e.g., the need for change, fear of facing up to oneself, etc.

Another major issue in mid-life is sexuality; certainly, fears and the reality of impotence are a common problem in the middle-age man. Excessive use of alcohol and drugs, as well as increasing stress, are the commonest causes of impotence in the middle years, not aging, Perhaps 90 percent of chronic impotence is due to psychological and not organic causes.

Insomnia is often a serious problem in the middle years. Anxiety, guilt, and anger may affect one's ability to sleep, and depression may cause early awakening. Depression and insomnia may be most frequently observed in hard-striving persons who are most subject to middle-life depressions.

Psychopathology of all types increases in both sexes in mid-life, as depression steadily increases in incidence. Pro-senile conditions may emerge in the fifties, and suicide rates rise. Also common in middle life are paranoid states and various forms of depression.

Mental illnesses most likely to occur in the middle-aged person are presenile psychoses, alcoholism, drug addiction, schizophrenic reactions, paranoid states, and depressions, most notably the manic-depressive reaction, especially the depressed type. Occurring only in the middle-aged person is involutional depression, an agitated type of depression which occurs in an individual who has premorbid personality characteristics of a compulsive or obsessive type, characteristics like perfectionism, overconscientiousness, and penuriousness.

What about therapy in middle age? Any prospect of therapy in middle age is based clearly on the possibility of change. Psychotherapy for the patient in mid-life does not have to be any different than for the patient of any other age. However, specific elements in therapy of the middle aged derive from the psychosocial and psychodynamic nature of mid-life. Hence, it is necessary to separate age-specific problems from personality problems; for example, psychotherapy of the middle aged, in the most general sense, is the psychotherapy of reevaluation (e.g., stock-taking) and possible redirection. Therapy's goal is to bring to consciousness an accurate appraisal of one's self so that one is in a position to elect changes or to stay essentially on course. Typically, there is a desire for some selective change.

Family therapy might aid in both the evaluation and the process of change and redirection. Particularly useful might be group therapy, and middle-aged people gain a good deal by working in groups composed of different age levels, diverse personality styles, and varied diagnoses.

Clearly, mental well-being is closely allied to physical well-being, and any improvement that can be made in the middle-age patient's physical condition and nutrition should be part of the psychotherapist's program.

Also, there should be help in the area of sexual difficulties, as it is well-accepted and documented that sex problems are a critical factor in marital difficulties. Work must be done on the development of mutuality and intimacy, but also direct work along the behavioral lines of Masters and Johnson might need to be done.

Therapy in middle age is not only a therapy of inventory and redirection, but also it is a therapy dealing with grief and restitution. It is highly necessary to raise a person's awareness of age changes and to help to develop a vigorous acceptance, rather than resignation or a counterphobic reaction. At any age successful psychoanalysis depends on reaching some realistic resolution of reality of one's own death.

In mid-life also there might be a restyling of income maintenance in order to mitigate the fears of an insecure old age. Providing day-care centers for old people, as well as for children, would provide greater freedom to the middle aged, and there should be massive public educational programs to reform diet, reduce alcoholism, and encourage physical fitness.

Education beginning in grammar school could help to prepare individuals to enjoy their leisure time.

Education beginning in grammar school could help to prepare people to enjoy leisure; therefore, the so-called minor subjects of music, art, etc., could well be major subjects. *Throughout* life there should be life cycle education, and this will have great significance for the religious educator.

Faith of Middle-Aged Adults

This discussion will now direct itself to one of mid-life's great possibilities and qualities. The psychologist Carl Jung (1938) initially drew attention to this great possibility and quality; the spiritual dimensions that can accompany middle age. Jung discovered in his psycho-analytic practice that the years after forty provided an ideal opportunity to deepen spiritual and religious values by reflecting on the meaning of life and death; in Jung's view, religion aided persons in becoming individuated or integrated by providing a unifying philosophy of life (p. 65). Erik Erikson (1978) followed Jung's lead in perceiving a potentially quite positive role for religion throughout the life cycle, but particularly in later life. Erikson described the psycho-social crisis of mid-life as a choice between generativity or stagnation or self-absorption (p. 7). This crisis, Erikson says, is resolved through loving care which he defines as "the widening concern for what has been generated by love or accident" (p. 131).

Though Erikson's delineation of mid-life crisis has received general acceptance, several psychologists have added to his description. R. Peck in 1955 presented four related crises in the middle years. First, adults in mid-life must learn to value wisdom over the physical prowess they may have had in earlier life. Second, adults in their relationships must come to see the value of all forms of social contact and move beyond considering only sexual elements as important in human relationships. Third, adults need to develop an emotional flexibility which enables them to forge other relationships when parents die and children leave the home. A fourth crisis or final task is avoiding mental rigidity by developing a mental flexibility which gives people the power to assimilate and accommodate new questions and answers.

Peck's research does not explicitly treat the religious dimensions of life, although his research certainly has implications for understanding religious development, as this chapter will indicate later. The same can certainly be said for D. Levinson's research; Levinson places the mid-life transition at age forty. Early adulthood ends at this time, and middle adulthood begins.

Levinson sees four tasks or polarities encountered at this time, polarities which need resolution. Jung's influence can clearly be seen in a description of these polarities. Persons have to resolve the young/old polarity by neither clinging too tenaciously to youth nor becoming prematurely aged. The second polarity between destruction and creation must be faced by accepting the dark side of personality: sin, death, suffering, destructiveness, and guilt. The masculine/feminine polarity must be integrated in individuals by an acceptance of power with feeling. The final polarity is attachment/separation, which must be balanced throughout life, but especially at this time. Levinson designates religion as an example of this polarity; religion must become more personal for adults as they become detached from dependence on the religion in which they were socialized.

Levinson concludes his mid-life treatment by indicating

how the life structure of individuals is modified at this time. Middle-aged adults become mentors to younger adults. Also, changes take place at this time within marriage, especially middle-class marriages, with women becoming more free and assertive.

What the adult religious educator misses in the adult development research is explicit attention to the religious dimensions of human development in mid-life. G. Vaillant (1977), for one, has directed attention to the religious dimension in his follow-up study of men who were college students between 1939-1942. The major focus of his study is an analysis of various mechanisms these men used in coping with life problems. Vaillant places generativity at the heart of mid-life crisis and designates it as a second adolescence. During their fifties many men developed a capacity to care for others that they did not previously believe possible.

Vaillant also discovered a modal pattern in the religious development of these men studied. He explains the reappearances of religion in the fifties of these men as the rediscovery of internalized parents. Vaillant accepts as an apt description of adult development the very Christian metaphor of "pilgrim's progress." Adult religious development, in this metaphor, depends on mysterious growth within the person which is inspired by equally mysterious forces outside the person.

E. Jacques (1965) is one writer who provides a possible explanation for the renewed interest in religion in the fifties. Jacques contends that the mid-life crisis is a reaction which occurs not only in creative geniuses like Bach, Michelangelo, et al., but in everyone. Fundamentally, it is the painful awareness that one will die which causes this crisis. Certainly, in mid-life the awareness that one's parents are aging, together with one's children maturing, contributes to the feeling that it is one's turn next to age and die.

It is quite clear that Jacques does not consider increased religious concerns in this period of life as healthy responses to mid-life crises. However, what he proposes as healthy responses—living life with conscious knowledge of eventual death, accepting death as an integral part of living, and a heightened capacity for love and affection and human insight—can all be found in sound religious experience.

A more explicitly religious treatment of religious development in middle life can be found in James Fowler's theory of faith development. Fowler's description of this faith stage presents the highest ideals of religious life which are found in nearly all religious traditions. However, what may be essential in the area of faith development research are more descriptive studies of faith stories and religious journeys of individuals, with a limited amount of philosophical and theological interpretations of faith development. Therefore, it is evident that though theories such as Fowler's shed some light on religious development dynamics, a preferable model for study would be theories of psychosocial development that treat a plenitude of human development dimensions.

The social psychologist Paul Maves (1971) has presented a fruitful approach to the study of adult development in one's middle years. Maves' approach to adult religious development is sensitive to the social and environmental forces that influence religious life. Maves contends that "religion as a dimension of experience or behavior response is integrally related to the total structure of the personality, so that changes in religious belief, attitudes, or behavior are subject to the conditions which determine changes in any other area of life" (p. 783).

Maves concedes that studies concerning religious development in adulthood are at an early stage, and he reports that religion in these studies is correlated with other personality dimensions as an integral part of the total picture of responses. However, Maves' theory of the importance of environmental factors as determinative of changes in adult life has yet to be tested.

Clearly, the study of religious development in middle adult years is and has been a fruitful area for researchers, and the insights of those who have worked with adults in these years are also of great value. The interest that adults in mid-life have expressed in such religious movements as Marriage Encounter, Charismatic Renewal, Bible Prayer and Study Groups indicates a spiritual interest and hunger that is attributable to both psychological and cultural factors. In most religious groups it is mid-life adults who are the most active members in worship, education, and service programs.

Faith of Older Adults

It is only a logical step to direct discussion of this chapter from mid-life adulthood to life and faith of older adults. As with the spiritual dimensions of mid-life, Jung (1933) was the first psychologist to direct attention to life's advanced years. Jung noted that deep-seated changes took place within the human psyche in old age and suggested that in life's advanced years individuals turn inward to find a meaning and a wholeness in life that would make it possible to accept death as the end of life. In Jung's perspective older persons need future goals to age successfully, and he suggested this is the ultimate reason why all great religions have offered hope in an afterlife so as to enable older persons to cope with pain, suffering, and death.

However, advanced age has still not received the same amount or degree of attention from developmental psychologists as have adulthood's first two stages. For example, the research of eminent people like Levinson and Gould does *not* include stages of development into life's latter years. This period of life, however, has been studied by other types of psychologists and social scientists.

One focus of research on older adulthood concerns theories of successful aging. For example, R. A. Kalish (1975, p. 60) presents a number of theories on successful aging. One view is that older persons age successfully when they adopt a way of life that is considered *socially desirable* for their age group. A second theory suggests that successful aging is related to the maintenance of *middle-age activities.* A third view is that persons age successfully if they have a sense of *satisfaction with their present status* and activities. The final view states that successful aging comes from *a feeling of satisfaction with one's life.*

Both psychological and sociological evidence points to the conclusion that religious faith can be a strong force in the latter part of life. Religion will have meaning in old age commensurate to the degree to which it had meaning in life's earlier stages. However, and this is a crucial point, the elderly's religious faith will have a different emphasis and perspective. In old age perspectives on faith are open to persons that were not really available when they were younger. Hence, older people have the potential to see deeply into the fundamental truths of religious faith. They can attain an appreciation of the positive role of suffering, and as people become older, they become ever more aware of their dependence on others. This reality allows the great opportunity for insight into the fundamental creatureliness that we have in our relationship with God. Also, it is usually only at the end of life and facing suffering and death that people come to a complete realization of the central religious mystery of death and resurrection.

Social science tells us that the individuals who have religious faith and a tight-knit community of people to support them and care for them are the people who best face death's inexorability and inevitability. A religious body or group can furnish this care and support for individuals who might not have the support of a family or friendship group. Clearly, it is easier for the elderly to experience God's acceptance if this acceptance is mediated through a loving community. In advanced age, persons have the potential of reaching the maturest form of prayer, which is acceptance of God and openness to his love.

One of the definite findings on successful aging is that continued activities contribute to happiness, and in later life people may have many opportunities for activities which express the charity and love preached within all religious bodies. However, one of the dangers that older persons face is a disgust with life that Erikson, for example, contrasts with integrity. Advanced age is replete with a myriad of small opportunities to display the courage and the love that dispel disgust and produce integrity. It is with courage and love that people are able to accept both the sufferings and joys of old age.

Conclusion

This discussion has attempted a rather difficult task: describing the faith journey of individuals from mid-life to old age. This writer has relied mainly on theories and research of the social sciences. Social science often takes as its task the examining of conventional wisdom, including that of religious tradition. Though many social scientists have examined human development without considering, indeed even ignoring, the religious dimension, an ever increasing number of researchers have begun to look explicitly at religious development as an integral part of human development.

The adult religious educator can benefit considerably from a knowledge of adult development studies. The function of adult religious educators is to determine what areas of adult development need special treatment from a religious point of view. This can be achieved by an examination of the area under discussion and by a needs assessment of members of the religious body. The religious teachings of religious bodies can certainly not be ignored, yet these are not psychologically and educationally the best starting points or organizational principles around which to develop programs. The actual challenge is to begin where people experience themselves to be and to shed light on their problems and tasks both from religious sources and other sources.

Though a knowledge of adult development is essential for adult religious educators, this knowledge can be supplemented beneficially by an understanding of how adults learn. A significant body of literature has developed in the last few decades which provides useful generalizations for adult religious educators in determining the types of educational experiences that should be provided for different groups of adults.

As we have indicated throughout this chapter, loneliness is not a major or recurring theme in the lives of the middle-aged individuals. This is attested to by even the most cursory review of the available clinical and educational literature. However, one of the central functions of education is prevention—a concept often overlooked by educators.

The educational needs of the middle-aged adult combined with the "intimations of mortality" suggest that middle-aged persons may be in an optimum position to innoculate themselves and others against the ravages of loneliness. Further, for those adults who experience chronic loneliness, middle age is often the "crunch" point at which the situation may become inaccessible.

Many issues touch the life of the middle-aged person quite directly. They include:

1. Increasingly frequent losses of older friends and relatives, etc.
2. Grief reactions as parents die.
3. Sexual dysfunction often manifested as impotence in the male and inhibition in the female.
4. Depression as one reviews one's life in a search for a fuller expression of personal dreams and goals. In short, the person becomes acutely aware for the first time that there is more time behind him than ahead of him!

The religious and ethical educator may approach the problem of loneliness in middle age much as a therapist approaches clinical intervention. Like psychotherapy, the educational process would be focused on reevaluation and redirection of one's life.

Reflection and contemplation as well as a survey of one's life can be a central point of educational intervention. Within the concept of growing accountability and integration of the disparate elements in one's life, the religious educator may help individuals target the areas of their lives that need help and redirection. What emerges is often striking: Some individuals are very lonely and on the road to chronic isolation, but they never think about it or focus on it because they are too busy meeting the demands of others. The religious educator can here suggest time for reflection and integration as well as action. If one is isolated, the educator can enable the person to develop more effective social skills and to become injected into the life of the community.

It is painfully obvious that individuals often have never taken the time to reevaluate their lives and redirect them. To encourage this evaluation, the religious educator might direct attention to the exploration of the concept and experience of fidelity. As indicated earlier in this chapter, fidelity is a critical issue of mid-life. One finds that individuals who report isolation and loneliness have been *rigid* rather than faithful. By this I mean they have handled their life commitments (to spouse, family, church, etc.) as though they were once-for-all. There seems to be in these individuals no sense of fidelity as an *active* process which must be renewed and vitalized. Often these individuals' isolation and loneliness are a reflection of the fact that they have been "doing the actions" without the concomitant vitalization and rewards.

These feelings of nonvitality often lead people to desire to streamline their communications. In short, companionship, friendship, etc., have been sufficiently unrewarding that many people tend to withdraw from new contacts as well as eschewing more traditional associations. This may not have an immediate impact but the long-term result is deadly: isolation and loneliness. Before individuals become "old," the religious educator is in a prime position to involve these people in group activities within the parish. As a result of shared experiences, individuals can become aware of the universality of their experiences as well as the need for support (to give and take) and empathy.

We know from the religious needs and beliefs of the middle-aged person that certain themes and needs predominate. The religious educator may well direct his/her interventions toward the major themes of middle-age as argued by Peck (1955). These include focusing on the need to go beyond physical ability and begin to appreciate the role of wisdom, as well as approaching people in more flexible ways. This flexibility can be directly assessed by the religious educator as he/she begins exploring alternate visions of God, religious experience, etc. This task will directly involve the teacher in arranging situations where the students can accommodate and assimilate new points of view. The ability to contain rigidity and to continue to engage in autoplastic and alloplastic adaptation is the educational *sine qua non* of successful coping with loneliness. It is no accident that people who have become "old and miserable," when looked at closely, were once "middle-aged and miserable" as well. The religious educator has the opportunity to intervene here and to empower individuals to explore, adapt, and change. As we will discuss later in the chapter on older adults, the group process will be a potent tool to achieve these goals.

The religious educator will have his/her hands full. Middle-aged people often want to "go back" to the faith of an earlier day as a remedy, but the fact as known by educators is that nothing stays the same. Everything changes. There is no going back since nothing stands still. The religious educator will have to enhance the individuals' skills in moving forward. This forward momentum requires a willingness and adaptability (or susceptibility) to change which, in itself, requires assimilation and accommodation. The deft religious educator will use the communal/group experience to assure that each individual encounters both aspects of human growth. Such flexibility and growth preclude isolation and loneliness.

References

Allport, G. *Becoming: Basic considerations for a psychology of personality.* New Haven, Conn.: Yale University Press, 1955.

Bouwsma, W. Christian adulthood. In E. Erikson (Ed.), *Adulthood*. New York: Norton, 1978.

Erikson, E. *Insight and responsibility.* New York: Norton 1964.

Erikson, E. Reflections on Dr. Borg's life cycle. In E. Erikson (Ed.), *Adulthood.* New York: Norton, 1978.

Fowler, J. Stages in faith development. In T. Hennessy (Ed.), *Values and moral development.* New York: Paulist Press, 1977.

Fowler, J. Stage six and the kingdom of God. *Religious Education,* 75(3), May-June, 1980.

Fowler, J. *Stages of faith.* New York: Harper & Row, 1981.

Fowler, J., et al. *Life maps: Conservations on the journey of faith.* Waco, Tex.: Word Books, 1978.

Fromm, E. *The anatomy of human destructiveness.* New York: Fawcett, 1973.

Jacques, E. Death and the mid-life crisis. *International Journal of Psychoanalysis,* 1965, 46, 502-514.

Jung, C. G. The stages of life. In C. Jung, *Modern man in search of a soul.* New York: Harcourt, 1933.

Jung, C. *Psychology and religion.* New Haven, Conn.: Yale University Press, 1938.

Kalish, R. A. *Late adulthood: Perspective on human development.* Monterey, Calif.: Brooks/Cole, 1975.

Levinson, D., and Associates. *The seasons of a man's life.* New York: Ballantine, 1978.

Maslow, A. *Religions, values, and peak experiences.* Columbus: Ohio State University Press, 1964.

Maves, P. Religious development in adulthood. In M. Sterommen (Ed.), *Research on religious development.* New York: Hawthorn, 1971.

Peck, R. Psychological developments in the second half of life. In B. Neugarten (Ed.), *Middle age and aging.* Chicago: University of Chicago Press, 1955.

Vaillant, G. *Adaptation to life.* Boston: Little, Brown, 1977.

Chapter 6

Experience of Loneliness and Old Age

Definition of Aging

Current literature supplies numerous definitions of aging. Since the process of aging may be conceived from various perspectives, the subsequent definition becomes a function of that particular view. I favor a concept of aging consistent with the definition set forth by Birren and Renner (1977). They define aging as, "the regular behavior changes that occur in mature genetically representative organisms living under representative environmental conditions as they advance in chronological age" (p. 5).

We can further refine the definition by distinguishing between biological, psychological, and social age. Biological age is the individual's physical status in relation to his/her life expectancy. Psychological age refers to the adaptive behavioral capabilities of the individual in relation to other individuals. Social age deals with social roles the individual plays as well as social habits developed and must be judged in terms of societal expectations for the individual's age.

Changes in biological, psychological, and social age are not necessarily parallel within the individual, nor are these patterns similar from individual to individual. Direction and rate of change may vary for each of the three components. Decline or growth in one area is not necessarily associated with a proportional decline or growth in another area. It is therefore possible to experience a decline in physical status while simultaneously experiencing positive growth in psychological adaptive capabilities.

Factors Which Contribute to Loneliness in Old Age

Biological Correlates of Aging

As a biological process, aging is characterized by a decline in functioning which ultimately terminates with death. It is "progressive loss of functional capacity after an organism has reached maturity" (Busse & Blazer, 1980; p. 4). There is a deterioration in major organs and systems; heart, lungs, kidneys, liver, nervous and digestive systems lose their former capabilities. The immune system weakens and the individual no longer resists disease with his/her previous strength. This results in "declines in mobility, energy, strength, and stress tolerance" (Yurick et al., 1980; p. 5).

How prevalent are physical limitations in the elderly compared with the total population? In 1980 there were 31.4 million individuals with an activity limitation due to chronic physical disorders (selected chronic conditions include heart conditions, arthritis and rheumatism, hypertention, impairment of back/spine, and impairment of lower back extremities and hips (Statistical, p. 85). Of this total, 10.2 million were under forty-five years of age, 10.4 million were between the ages of forty-five and sixty-four, and 10.8 million were sixty-five years of age or older. Although persons age sixty-five and older accounted for approximately 11 percent of the total population in 1980, they accounted for over one third of all cases of activity limitation due to chronic illness.

Perhaps a more meaningful comparison is the percentage of the population with no impairment. Of the total population, 85.6 percent are not limited by a physical condition, while 54.8 percent of those sixty-five years and older enjoy this freedom. The contrast is heightened if we examine individuals forty-five years and younger. In this case, a full 93.2 percent are free from the debilitating effects of physical impairment.

Although it is true that the majority of those sixty-five and over are in good health (if we define good health as the absence of an activity limitation), it is also true that the elderly experience substantially more restrictions based on poor health than the population in general. Logically we can deduce that the increased isolation due to physical limitation contributes to the experience of loneliness in old age. Kivett (1978 and 1979) provides support for this assumption in two separate studies. She classified 103 rural widows into three levels of loneliness: frequently lonely, sometimes lonely, and never lonely. She found that physical isolation as determined by self-perceived health and availability of transportation separated those who were frequently lonely from those who were never lonely. In the second study, Kivett classified 418 rural elderly into either high or low risks for loneliness. Poor vision and self-rated health were two of seven conditions which were associated with frequent loneliness. (The other conditions were widowhood, problems with transportation, frequent use of telephone, low participation in organized social activities, and being female). Poor health has also been found to account for conditions related to loneliness. Mussen, Honzik, and Eichorn (1982) found that poor health was associated with a lack of life satisfaction in elderly men. Likewise, Markides and Martin (1979) and Beck (1982) found life satisfaction and happiness to be strongly associated with good health in the elderly.

Developmental Views of Aging

As early as 1933, Jung saw the later half of life as a process of turning inward toward the self. To deal with one's impending death an individual must, to some degree, remove himself from the world. In his introspection he develops a philosophical or religious view of life and death (p. 55).

Erikson (1959; p. 87) views the life cycle as a series of stages which have specific goals. In the last stage the individual must attain ego integrity by turning inward, examining his life, and accepting it as it has been lived. If the individual cannot develop a sense of integrity from past accomplishments, but instead focuses on past mistakes and missed opportunities, despair results. Perhaps the most extensive work on the theme of turning inward has been proposed by Cumming and Henry (1961). Based on their study of a healthy cross-section of the elderly in Kansas City, they introduced a concept which has been known as disengagement. Disengagement theory holds that the elderly person withdraws and detaches himself, gradually reducing contacts and involvements with the larger society. This is seen as a natural, adaptive process which is necessary because of the elderly individual's impending death. Cumming and Henry viewed disengagement as a necessity for successful adaptation to old age.

Although subsequent research does not substantiate the disengagement process as a healthy adaptation to aging, it is difficult to point to a cause-and-effect relationship (Larson, 1978; p. 109). In other words, did the elderly turn inward in an effort to examine their life and values, or were they forced into passivity and isolation due to poor health? We might conclude that those who choose a contemplative lifestyle would be well-adjusted, while those who involuntarily withdrew would not. Unfortunately, most research to date has not separated the effects of these intervening variables.

Owens (1981, p. 113) feels that turning inward can indeed be beneficial in old age. She sees an absence of wholeness, expressed in the lack of integration of left and right hemispheres of the brain, as a cause of many difficulties experienced in old age. She proposes the use of meditation as a means by which attainment of wholeness is possible. Meditation allows the activation of previously buried virtues. It enables the individual to use these resources to deal with the problems of aging. By the process of meditative exploration, the "true self" is found. This true self paves the way for the "moment of becoming" when the individual experiences a oneness with the universe. Owens feels that meditators can find companionship in their awakened selves and in their experience of oneness with the universe. This companionship is a powerful aid in dealing with loneliness.

She states that meditation "transforms the whole hierarchy of values from the seen to the unseen. The chief riches valued by followers of the Eternal Way are inner wealth: certitude, courage, creativity, honesty, love, desire to serve others, selflessness, purity, and joy. We can conclude, therefore, that turning inward can be beneficial in dealing with problems of old age if it is utilized as a development of psychological resources. Removing oneself for the purposes of solitary contemplation, be it expressed as meditation or prayer, can be a positive experience in old age. If the individual uncovers previously obscured inner resources, withdrawal can be comforting and productive.

The Role of Sociocultural Factors

Despite an increased awareness and acceptance of the aging process in recent years, ageism continues to exist in American society and is one factor contributing to the experience of loneliness in old age (Butler, 1969; p. 243). Alex Comfort (1980) speaks of the cultural problem termed gerontophobia. He states that, "unique to our culture is its rejection of the old, their exclusion from work and their accustomed social space, their premature burial as 'unpeople,' and a rich and erroneous folklore of mental decline, infirmity, diminished sexuality, ineducability, and the normality of causeless mental disorders in the old" (p. 2).

Changes in chronological age are typically accompanied by changes in social roles. At earlier points in the lifecycle, loss of one role is usually substituted by another. For example, a college student will, upon graduation, lose the role of "student." However, it is likely that this role will be replaced with "employee." A young couple may no longer consider themselves "newlyweds" after the birth of their first child. They have, however, now acquired a new role: that of parents. The difference between this type of situation and that of the elderly revolves around the issue of replacement.

When an elderly person retires, the work role is frequently not replaced with another job. Loss of employment is often accompanied by a loss in economic security and social status. The individual can no longer define himself as an employee of XYZ Company. Contributing to loneliness may be a loss of contact with coworkers and friends. Unlike the young person who has the opportunity to replace this job with another, the elderly individual's role loss is permanent.

Another frequent role change experienced by the elderly is that of marital status. With increasing age, the loss of spouse through death becomes more probable. The widowed individual loses much more than an identity; he loses a lifelong partner, a companion, and a primary source of psychological support. Due to lack of time and opportunity, remarriage (replacement) becomes less likely. This type of unreplaced role loss is not universal, nor has it always been the case.

Gutmann (1980) feels that certain types of societies are more suited to supporting the mental health of the elderly than others. According to Gutmann, the small, face-to-face, traditional folk society comes closest to providing optimal support for the elderly. Hareven (1978) also supports this general view. She feels that the negative image of old age and consequent isolation of the elderly from the mainstream of society are a function of increasing segregation of different life stages in modern American society. She points out that "the absence of dramatic transitions to adult life allowed a more intensive interaction among different age groups within the family and the community, thus providing a greater sense of community and interdependence among people at various stages in the life course" (p. 208).

Although both Gutmann and Hareven concur on the type of social structure most supportive of the elderly, Gutmann proposes a somewhat different perspective on causation. He states that "there appears to be an assured, organic linkage—a 'deep structure'—that bonds the older traditional persons and the sacred systems of their culture as these are represented in theology, in myth, and in ritual. This special bonding between the sacred and the geriatric leads to traditional gerontocracy, to special privilege and esteem for the aged, based on their special access to spiritual resources" (p. 433). A loss of isolation causes a redistribution of power within the previously insulated society. The introduction of new ideas weakens the strength of the old. Economic power is now accessible from sources other than familiar holdings. The power base shifts from within the culture to an outside source. Gutmann distinguishes between urbanization and modernization, stating that the former is not necessarily a product of the latter. In modernization, a different culture is accepted as better than that of the present one. If, however, both rural and urban areas are part of the same social evolution, harmony of process is achieved. Before their contact with the West, Oriental cities preserved traditional values, rituals, and practices. It is therefore theoretically possible to maintain a supportive social structure for the elderly in modern urban society.

Gutmann proposes a creative solution to a very difficult problem. He points out that certain secular professions— for example, law, medicine, and academia—might create the essence of the earlier religious function of the elderly. Appointing older practitioners to represent the ethical standards of the profession would effectively recreate the sacred status of the aged.

These professions resemble folk society by sharing a strong distinction between the sacred and the secular. The younger members would address the routine norms of practice while the elderly would address the moral issues. Because the elder is no longer motivated by self-interest in building his own career, he can be a more objective spokesman for the ethical position. The elder's function would therefore be of value to society and also be supportive of the social status and mental health of the aged in modern society.

Situational Factors and Loneliness in Old Age

Retirement and Income

Although one might expect retirement to be correlated with loneliness and have an overall detrimental effect in old age, this is not always the case. There are several intermediate and interconnected conditions which determine whether or not retirement has an adverse effect on the elderly.

Income is a significant determinant of the evaluation of retirement. Beck (1982) found that lower income was one of the main determinants in a negative evaluation of retirement. In March of 1982 the median annual income for all persons in the United States was $19,074. For those aged sixty-five and over, the median annual income was only $9,903. Over 20 percent of the elderly have annual incomes under $5,000 (Statistical Abstracts, pp. 82-83).

To the extent that low income reduces opportunities, status, and the overall quality of life, and to the extent that retirement results in a reduction in income, we can conclude that retirement has an adverse effect on the elderly.

The state of the elderly individual's health is another significant factor in the overall evaluation of retirement (Beck, 1982). Poor health is associated with a negative evaluation of retirement and limits mobility and opportunities.

A significant determinant of good adjustment to retirement, and the area which offers the most constructive avenues for possible change, is the extent to which the retired individual has substitute satisfactions available (Botwinick, 1978; p. 82). Meaningful volunteer work for the elderly has been proposed as one such substitute. Hunter and Linn (1980-81) compared retired elderly volunteers with nonvolunteers and found that volunteers had a significantly higher degree of life satisfaction, a stronger will to live, and fewer psychologically maladaptive symptoms (depression, anxiety, somatization). Palmore (1980, p. 236) proposes that religious institutions (churches, synagogues) may offer a fruitful alternative for a previous work role. Religious institutions are a logical place where elders can assume meaningful roles within the organization because they are the community institutions to which elders most frequently belong. Because, in all likelihood, the elderly have been lifelong members, a sense of continuity is provided as well.

Living Situation

Although living alone does not necessarily imply a higher level of loneliness it seems logical that physical aloneness might predispose the individual to a higher risk of loneliness. The elderly are more likely than other age group to reside by themselves. In 1981, persons sixty-five years or older comprised 39.5 percent of all individuals living alone (Statistical Abstracts, pp. 82-83). Cohen (1980) points out that living alone reduces the availability of an immediate source of social support and interaction. The lack of this social support is detrimental to healthy psychological adjustment.

The areas in which older individuals tend to reside further exacerbate possible loneliness. The elderly live alone in rural or urban settings more frequently than younger individuals (Hendricks & Hendricks, 1977). In rural settings, people become isolated by physical distance. Fear of crime may impose a need for self-imposed isolation on the urban elderly.

The author has excluded the institutionalized elderly from the discussion up to this point because, contrary to popular belief, only a small portion of the elderly reside in nursing homes and similar institutions (Ingram, 1977; pp. 303-308). Here the possibility for experiencing loneliness as a function of living situation increases. Dudley and Hillery (1977) report that alienation and lack of freedom are more frequent for nursing home residents than any other type of institutional residents.

Death of Spouse and Peers

It is an indisputable fact that the probability of loss of a spouse and peers increases as an individual advances in years. Although both sexes are more likely to be widowed as they age, women are much more likely to experience the loss of a spouse through death than men. In 1981, the percent of males widowed was as follows: age 55-64—4.1 percent, age 64-74—8.2 percent, age 75 and over—22.1 percent. For women the respective percentages were 18.4. 40.1, and 68.2 percent (Statistical Abstract)

The most common psychological disorder in old age is depression (Comfort, 1980). Depression is linked with loss, including the loss of a significant other (Steur, 1982). Loss of a spouse through death increases the risk of mortality for the surviving spouse (Epstein et al., 1975; Payne, 1975). Loneliness is among the various problems associated with the death of a spouse (Kivett, 1979). Paul Tillich (1980) states that the loneliness felt as a result of separation or death is the most widespread type of loneliness. The feeling of loss is heightened because the intimacy, contact, and communication experienced with these individuals helped us forget that we are alone. It is to this type of loneliness that formal religion most frequently addresses itself. The Judeo-Christian tradition offers solace to the bereaved with the hope for eternal life. The loss and loneliness experienced as a result of death can be viewed as temporary. Both the Hebrew and Christian scriptures reassure the reader of the worth of the human soul and convey the certitude of a life after death.

An alternate approach to the problems of death and loneliness is offered in Zen Buddhism (Keefer, 1980; p. 147). Both the experience of loneliness and the fear of death are results of the illusion of "self." The "self" is merely a collection of beliefs, tastes, and desires and can be abandoned. Experience itself is value neutral although characterized by duality. Life and death therefore, are simply dualities of one type of experience. The same holds true for loneliness and a sense of belonging. According to Zen these dualities may be experienced as painful or joyous at any particular point in time but contain no intrinsic value in and of themselves. They are simply part of the natural complexity of human existence.

Productive Solutions to the Problem of Loneliness in Old Age

Types and Variations of Loneliness

It is helpful to realize that loneliness is not a single entity and that productive solutions to the problem of loneliness will depend on the type of loneliness being addressed.

A general definition of loneliness is proposed by Jacob Landau (1980). He states that "loneliness means to feel our apartness, our inability to bridge the gaps that exist or may arise between ourselves and others" (p. 498). Keefer puts forth the following definition of loneliness: "I think, rather, that feelings of loneliness occur only when a person experiences deprivation of emotional gratification, and the deprivation is perceived to result from the inability of the lonely one to communicate his or her need to another being or other things" (p. 426).

Finally, an excellent general definition of loneliness is also proposed by Rubenstein and Shaver (1982). To them, "loneliness warns us that important psychological needs are going unmet. Loneliness is a healthy hunger for intimacy and community—a natural sign that we are lacking companionship, closeness, and a meaningful place in the world" (p. 2).

Landau (1980) further differentiates the concept of loneliness into social and individual loneliness. Of the two types of loneliness, social loneliness, according to Landau, is inherently soluble. Although it is experienced on an individual psychological level, it stems from social conditions and transactions. Individual loneliness however, is more difficult to conquer. It can be termed existential and can only be overcome by a recovery of lost cosmic interconnectedness.

These two conceptions of loneliness are not mutually exclusive. It is often difficult to draw the line between one type of loneliness and the other. However, in the most elementary sense, we can conceive solutions to social loneliness by a movement toward others, while existential loneliness must first be conquered by a movement toward the self. After the self has been discovered we find that movement toward others naturally follows. The distinction between the two types of loneliness might very well explain the often contradictory results of research in the area. Although the bulk of research equates healthy adjustment in old age to be highly correlated with the level of social interaction, this does not necessarily disprove the earlier developmental theories of Jung (1933), Erikson (1959), or Cumming and Henry (1961) who equate satisfactory adjustment in old age with a turning inward toward the self. It is quite possible that we are dealing with two types or levels of adjustment. The differentiation between healthy introspection and pathological withdrawal was not made or measured.

This leads us to a rather paradoxical distinction between loneliness and solitude. Although loneliness is often experienced as a consequence of isolation it is not necessarily equated with the state of being alone. It also follows that one may feel lonely despite social interaction. According to Rubenstein and Shaver (1982), "solitude is a kind of positive aloneness. And, paradoxically, solitude can be a corrective for prolonged loneliness" (p. 15). How can solitude be a productive solution to the problem of loneliness? Rubenstein and Shaver feel it is because of the relationship between active solitude and intimacy. They state, "in solitude we are intimate with ourselves in a way that enhances our intimacy with other people" (p. 176).

Psychological and Spiritual Growth

The concept of aging proposed by Birren and Renner (1977) was described earlier. This definition focused on changes experienced by the individual and was not limited to deterioration or decline. The elderly can experience both growth and decline in various areas of functioning. The aged have the capacity for growth and adaptation in the spiritual psychological area even though physical functioning may decline. This concept of aging is surprisingly similar to the Christian view of adulthood (Bouwsma, 1978; p. 55).

This view is not concerned with chronological differences among individuals: The Christian life is perceived as a process of growth, and all people are equal to the extent that they are growing spiritually or stagnating. The Christian way of life implies the experience of challenge and struggle. The Christian adult is not to avoid these challenges but rather to experience them and grow spiritually as a result. Possibilities for growth are indefinite and the process continual. The special problems of old age can therefore be viewed as opportunities for further spiritual and psychological growth.

Self-Concept and Healthy Adjustment to Aging

"Self-concept refers to the cognitive aspects of self-perception and consists of individuals' perceptions of themselves" (George, 1980). It relates to self-esteem which "refers to the affective and evaluative aspects of self-perception and consists of judgments made about the self as an object" (p. 114).

A comprehensive survey of individuals over sixty-five was conducted by Harris and Associates (1975). It was found that 56 percent of those over sixty-five years of age felt they were as happy now as when they were younger. This suggests that the majority of the elderly have a positive self-concept. However, a large percentage may not feel this way. One must realize that self-concept is a continuous process. The individual tends to maintain a self-concept consistent with that which was held in earlier years (Brubaker & Powers, 1976). In other words, if the individual had a positive self-concept before old age, it is likely that this positive self-concept will be maintained. The same holds true for a negative self-concept.

Many of the changes which accompany old age have been discussed. Several offer a potentially detrimental effect on self-concept. Failing health, a reduction of income, loss of friends and family, and loss of work role—all of these changes threaten a positive self-concept. Yet many elderly can and do maintain a positive self-concept. Research has shown that certain conditions correlate with a positive adjustment to aging.

One of these correlates is the maintenance of an inner

directedness. Mancini (1980-81) has shown that locus of control was positively correlated with higher life satisfaction. This association was maintained even when controlling for other variables such as income and self-rated health. Reid et al. (1977) also confirm this association. They found that those with a negative self-concept tended to be less in control and less happy than those with a positive self-concept. Gutmann (1978) conducted an exploratory study of 410 elderly subjects, and he too confirmed the link between control and a positive self-concept. He found that action-taking was strongly associated with well-being in the aged.

The relationship between these findings and religious experience is clear. To the extent that prayer, solitude, or contemplation increases an awareness of self and promotes a greater degree of inner directedness, it will be related to a positive self-concept in old age. Those with a positive self-concept are much less likely to be lonely than those with a negative self-concept (Anderson et al., 1983).

Research overwhelmingly supports the view that social involvement enhances the maintenance of a positive self-concept, is associated with good adjustment to old age, and is negatively related to loneliness. Lopata (1980) interviewed over 1000 widows in the metropolitan Chicago area and found that the lonely lack social supports. They are also angry people who cannot draw emotional support from others. Rubenstein and Shaver (1982) analyzed approximately 30,000 surveys in their study of loneliness. They conclude that "the only lasting remedies for loneliness are mutual affection and participation in a genuine community" (p. 18). McClelland (1982) points to the importance of social interaction in the maintenance of a strong, positive self-concept and stresses that continued interaction is necessary to sustain it.

Snow and Crapo (1982) further confirm this association in their study of emotional bondedness in elderly medical patients. Emotional bondedness includes the sense that one receives support from another, the sense that there is mutual sharing with another, and the sharing of positive feelings with another. They studied over 200 aged ambulatory medical patients and concluded that emotional bondedness is positively related to health and subjective well-being.

On both the personal and institutional level, religious experience can foster a sense of community and belonging that counters loneliness and a negative self-concept (Staser & Staser, 1976). In fact, Kalish (1979) feels the absence of substantial numbers of elderly in traditional counseling settings may be explained by their utilization of the church for social and emotional support. He advocates the expansion of religious support services for the aged.

Perhaps the most significant problem in old age is that of loss. Loss frequently results in lowered self-esteem (Lazarus, 1980). Physical and interpersonal losses have been linked with psychopathology in the elderly (Blum & Tross, 1980; p. 148). The key to successful adaptation to loss appears to lie in the individual's ability to replace that loss (Wigdor, 1980; p. 257). On an individual level, religion may offer explanations for loss of comfort which lessen the degree and impact of loss. It may provide meaning to this painful experience. The teachings of most formal religions support altruism. Rubenstein and Shaver state that "altruism is an effective way out of loneliness. . . . Forget yourself for a while and attempt to help others. Paradoxically, you may solve your own problem in the process" (Rubenstein & Shaver, 1982; p. 184).

Rubenstein and Shaver highlight an essential ingredient in replacing loss—reaching out to others. Formal religious institutions are the community institutions to which elderly individuals most frequently belong. They provide an ideal medium by which the aged can reach out to others and replace losses with new social contacts. By becoming actively involved in the church, they can assume meaningful roles to replace other lost roles (work roles, social roles, etc.). In the process of reaching out to help others the elderly can ultimately help themselves.

References

Anderson, C. A., Horowitz, L. M., & French, R. Attritional style of lonely and depressed people. *Journal of Personality and Social Psychology*, 1983, 45 (1), 127-136.

Beck, S. H. Adjustment to and satisfaction with retirement. *Journal of Gerontology*, 1982, 37 (5), 616-624.

Birren, J. E. & Renner, V. J. Research on the psychology of aging: Principles and experimentation. In J. E. Birren & K. W. Schaie (Eds.), *Handbook of the psychology of aging*. Van Nostrand: New York, 1977.

Blum, J. E. & Tross, S. Psychodynamic treatment of the elderly: A review of issues in theory and practice. In Carl E. Eisendorfer (Ed.), *Annual Review of Gerontology & Geriatrics Vol. 1*. New York: Springer, 1980.

Botwinick, J. *Aging and behavior: A comprehensive integration of research findings*, 2nd ed. New York: Springer, 1978.

Bouwsma, W. J. Christian adulthood. In E. H. Erikson (Ed.), *Adulthood*. Norton: New York 1978.

Brubaker, T. H. & Powers, E. A. The stereotype of the old. *Journal of Gerontology*, 1976, 31, 441-447.

Busse, E. W. & Blazer, D. G. The theories and processes of aging. In Busse & Blazer (Eds.), *Handbook of geriatric psychiatry*. New York: Van Nostrand Reinhold, 1980.

Butler, R. Ageism: Another form of bigotry. *Gerontologist*, 1969, 9, 243.

Cohen, G. D. Prospects for mental health and aging. In J. E. Birren & R. B. Sloane (Eds.), *Handbook of mental health and aging*. Garden City, N.J.: Prentice-Hall, 1980.

Comfort, A. *Practice of geriatric psychiatry*. New York: Elsevier North Holland, 1980.

Cumming, E. & Henry, W. E. *Growing old*. New York: Basic Books, 1961.

Dudley, C. J. & Hillery, G. A. Freedom and alienation in homes for the aged. *Gerontologist*, 1977, 17(2), 140.

Epstein, G., Weitz, L., Roback, H., & McKee, E.A. Research on berea-
    vement: A selective critical review. *Comprehensive Psychiatry*, 1975, 16,
    537-546.
Erikson, E. H. Identity and the life cycle. *Psychological Issues Monograph
    I.* New York: International University Press, 1959.
George. L. K. *Role transitions in later life.* Monterey, Calif.: Brooks/Cole,
    1980.
Gutmann, D. Life events and decision making by older adults. *Gerontolo-
    gist*, 1978, 18 (5 part 1), 462-467.
Gutmann, D. Observations on culture and mental health in later life. In
    J. E. Birren & R. B. Sloane (Eds.), *Handbook of mental health and aging.*
    Englewood Cliffs, N.J.: Prentice-Hall, 1980.
Hareven, T. K. The last stage: Historical adulthood and old age. In
    E. H. Erikson (Ed.), *Adulthood.* New York: Norton, 1978.
Harris, L. & Associates. *The myth and reality of aging in America.* Washing-
    ton, D.C.: The National Council on Aging, 1975.
Hendricks, J. & Hendricks, C. D. *Aging in a mass society: Myths and
    realities.* Cambridge, Mass.: Winthrop, 1977.
Hunter, K. I. & Linn, M. W. Psychosocial differences between elderly
    volunteers and non-volunteers. *International Journal of Aging & Hu-
    man Development*, 1980-81, 12(3), 205-213.
Ingram, D. K. & Barry, J. R. National statistics on deaths in nursing
    homes: Interpretations and implications. *Gerontologist*, 1977, 17, 303-
    308.
Jung, C. G. *Modern man in search of a soul.* New York: Harcourt, 1933.
Kalish, R. The religious triad: Church, clergy, and faith in the resources
    network." *Generations*, Spring 1979, 3, 27.
Keefer, C. Loneliness and Japanese social structure. In Hartog, Audy,
    and Cohen (Eds.), *The anatomy of loneliness.* New York: International
    Universities Press, 1980.
Kivett, V. R. Discriminators of loneliness among the rural elderly: Impli-
    cations for intervention. *Gerontologist*, 1979, 19 (1), 108-115.
Landau, J. Loneliness and creativity. In Hartog, Audy, and Cohen
    (Eds.), *The anatomy of loneliness.* New York: International Universities
    Press, 1980.
Larson R. Thirty years of research on the subjective well-being of older
    Americans. *Journal of Gerontology*, 1978, 33, 109-29.
Lazarus, L. W. Self-psychology and psychotherapy with the elderly:
    Theory and practice. *Journal of Geriatric Psychiatry*, 1980, 13(1), 69-
    88.
Lopata, H. Z. Loneliness in widowhood. In Hartog, Audy, and Cohen
    (Eds.), *The anatomy of loneliness.* New York: International Universities
    Press, 1980.

Mancini, J. A. Effects of health and income on control orientation and life satisfaction among aged public residents. *International Journal of Aging and Human Development*, 1980-81, 12(3), 215-220.

Markides, K. S. & Martin H. W. A causal model of life satisfaction among the elderly. *Journal of Gerontology*, 1979, 34 (1), 86-93.

McClelland, K. Self-Conception and life satisfaction: Integrating aged subculture and activity theory. *Journal of Gerontology*, 1982, 37(6), 723-732.

Mussen P., Honzik, M. P., & Eichorn, D. H. Early adult antecedents of life satisfaction at age 70. *Journal of Gerontology*, 1982, 37 (3) 316-322.

Owens, C. M. Meditation as a solution to the problem of aging. In R. Kastenbaum (Ed.), *Old age on the new scene*. New York: Springer, 1981.

Palmore, E. The social factors in aging. In E. W. Busse & D. G. Blazer (Eds.), *Handbook of Geriatric Psychiatry*. New York: Van Nostrand Reinhold, 1980.

Payne, E. C. Depression and suicide. In J. G. Howell (Ed.), *Modern perspectives in psychiatry of old age*. New York: Brunner/Mazel, 1975.

Peterson, J. A. Social-psychological aspects of death and dying and mental health. In J. E. Birren & R. B. Sloane (Eds.), *Handbook of mental health and aging*. Englewood Cliffs, N.J.: Prentice-Hall, 1980.

Reid, D. W., Haas, G., & Harkings, D. Locus of desired control and positive self-concept of the elderly. *Journal of Gerontology*, 1977, 32(4), 441.

Rubenstein, C. & Shaver, P. *In search of intimacy*. New York: Delacorte Press, 1982.

Snow, R. & Crapo, L. Emotional bondedness, subjective well-being and health in elderly medical patients. *Journal of Gerontology*, 1982, 37(5), 609-615.

Staser, C. W. & Staser, H. T. Organized religion: Community considerations. In H. J. Oyer & J. Oyer (Eds.), *Aging and communication*. Baltimore: University Park Press, 1976.

Statistical Abstract of the United States, 1982-83, 103rd ed.

Steur, J. Psychotherapy for depressed elders. In D. G. Blazer (Ed.), *Depression in late life*. St. Louis: C. V. Mosby, 1982.

Tillich, P. Loneliness and solitude. In Hartog, Audy, & Cohen (Eds.), *The anatomy of loneliness*. New York: International Universities Press, 1980.

Wigdor, B. T. Drives and motivations with aging. In J. E. Birren & R. B. Sloane (Eds.), *Handbook of mental health and aging*. Englewood Cliffs, N.J.: Prentice-Hall, 1980.

Yurick, A. G., Robb, S. S., Spier, B. E., & Ebert, N. J. *The aged person and the nursing process*. New York: Appleton-Century-Crofts, 1980.

Chapter 7

Some Possible Approaches

Is there a case for loneliness as a topic of concern? That is an odd question for the end of a book on loneliness, but it is central to the topic. The body of literature is quite small. Peplau and Perlman (1982), in an attempt at a comprehensive search, have produced a bibliography of only 287 entries for the years 1932-1981 (pp. 407-417). There has been only a marginal growth since then. Investigators in the field readily agree that they cannot produce an unambiguous definition of loneliness. A comprehensive measuring tool has yet to be perfected. There are few theoretical models capable of generating testable hypotheses.

One cannot even speak with any assurance about loneliness as a universal, i.e., that everyone's loneliness has the same dynamics, or at least a cluster of dynamics from the same set. It may well be that loneliness is a misunderstood collective noun for two or more entirely different phenomena.

On the other hand, there is evidence that loneliness is a form of depression. If that is the case, then studying it in isolation from the body of knowledge that has been developed about depression is a most futile academic exercise.

Another unknown is the incidence of loneliness in our society. Too few studies exist under any definition of the

140

syndrome for a reasonable guess to be hazarded. A number of investigators have built an interesting case for a recent dramatic rise in the incidence of loneliness (Flanders, 1982; pp. 15-41). Although insightful, these hypotheses result from uncontrolled observations and rest upon assumptions about the social dynamics of the past.

Nevertheless, loneliness remains a serious and growing problem in our society. There are about 50 million single, divorced, or widowed people in the United States (Gordon, 1976; p. 216). Only a little reflection upon our society's typical concern for the elderly and upon the social awkwardness of being an unmarried mature adult will lead to the conclusion that loneliness is not a minor problem. An acceptance of the fact that some portion of the married population is also lonely only adds to the problem's magnitude.

If loneliness is so common (and I would make the case that it is a prevalent condition), why is it so unrecognized, so understudied, and so ill-understood? Loneliness is a problem that denies the validity of many of our most cherished cultural myths. Adults without partners in our society are judged to be failures (because they cannot find one) (Gordon, 1976; p. 37). Those who are incapable of intimacy are not "with it." Those who are without friends are losers. With the exception of the stereotypic shut-in, people who are lonely will deny their condition. Many only reluctantly admit it to themselves. For society to admit a widespread incidence of loneliness, it would have to face a questioning of the principles upon which it is organized. It is far easier to view lonely people as exceptions to the norm. It must be they who have failed; it cannot possibly be us.

It is not surprising that investigators cannot agree upon a definition of loneliness. It is a semantically slippery term.

Much of the difficulty stems from the fact that the term has been adopted from the lay vocabulary. Most technical terms are coined to describe a specific phenomenon and as such are neutral. In adopting "loneliness," we have unconsciously adopted with it our biased lay connotations.

The lay definition of "loneliness" carries with it a double presumption of deficiency. In lay terms, lonely people are people lacking in companionship. This phrasing overtly presumes that their condition ought to be corrected by the acquisition of friends. Its less obvious presumption is that the victims are to blame; people without a circle of companionship are losers. The lack friends because they are lacking within themselves.

The victims share this view although, interestingly enough, their focus is much narrower. Lonely adolescents and non-elderly adults think of themselves as individuals without partners and operate on the presumption that securing a partner will solve their problem (Gordon, 1976; pp. 37-38).

Another version of this bias in the examination of loneliness results from the historic accident that most of the observational literature on loneliness has been produced by sociologists, whose very discipline casts social isolates in a deficient light (Peplau and Perlman, 1982; p. 21).

The presumptive ascription of deficiency to loneliness hobbles most attempts at a scientific definition of the term. Weiss (1982) sees loneliness as being either a condition of emotional isolation or one of social isolation. He feels emotional isolation is produced by the absence of an attachment figure, while social isolation is produced by the absence of access to a social network (p. 74). Both definitions proscribe any remediation which does not remove the absence.

Young (1982) tries to avoid this trap by defining loneliness temporally. He classifies loneliness as either being short-term (transient or situational) or chronic, with chronic being limited to durations exceeding two years (pp. 382-383).

Young's approach "rests on the premise that loneliness, like depression, is in a large part a cognitive phenomenon: that is, the way individuals view relationships is perhaps the most important determinant of how satisfying their friendships are and therefore of how lonely they feel" (p. 379).

In this framework, Young treats chronic loneliness by first getting his patients to overcome their anxiety about spending time alone (p. 391). In doing so, he seems to avoid both a prescriptive definition and its suggested cure. However, his complete therapy involves five more mandatory steps, culminating with making "an emotional commitment to an appropriate partner for a relatively long period of time" (p. 391). Young is as caught up in the connotative semantics of loneliness as Weiss.

Mijuskovic (1977) avoids this trap by defining the alienation of loneliness as a basic psychological drive, one he ranks right behind food and shelter (pp. 113-114). Mijuskovic feels that the major expression of the unsatisfied state of this drive is boredom, and that it is a fear of confronting our fundamental loneliness that drives us to activity (work, hobbies) (p. 127). From this point of view, loneliness is not a pathological condition that can be cured with companionship, but an intrinsic part of being human (p. 120).

Mijuskovic's conjectures are as unsubstantiated as all of the other hypotheses about loneliness, and they need to be tested before they can form the basis for further speculation. But the drive hypotheses are seriously inadequate because they logically reduce to input + black box = output. Without an understanding of the black box, such hypotheses have little explanatory value.

However, Mijuskovic's hunches that loneliness is universal and that research, education, and therapy ought to focus on the individual as an entity (not just as part of a malfunctioning social system) have profound implications that investigators in the field ought to consider. For example, these implications have a tantalizing ability to explain such escapist behavior (see Flanders below). If Mijuskovic's hypotheses were proven substantially correct, one wonders what a person who had learned to face himself fully would be like and what a society of such individuals would be like.

The alternative to presuming loneliness to be intrinsic to the human condition is to characterize it as a condition experienced by only a portion of the population. However, without a theoretical model for loneliness, it is impossible to agree on what it is and what its manifestations are, or to measure its incidence within the population. A number of investigators have tried to develop identifying instruments—tests that will consistently measure the attributes or responses of lonely people—in the hope that these could be used to specify a definition of loneliness.

As Russell (1982), points out, these approaches have mainly succeeded in demonstrating that the theoretical underpinning has to come first (pp. 81-82). The instrumental results give no clue as to whether loneliness is one condition experienced by everyone who is lonely, or a cluster of conditions which different people experience in different or similar circumstances (pp. 97-98). Since there are no useful longitudinal studies, there are no objective data on whether loneliness manifests itself as an attitude or a trait or both (p. 90).

Nevertheless, some useful findings have been produced.

A number of investigators have hypothesized a correlation between loneliness and a lack of self-esteem, and Peplau et al. (1982) found quantifiable evidence of one (pp. 143-147). Unfortunately, correlations beg both the question of causality and that of its direction.

Another interesting finding is a close relationship between loneliness and depression, although there is some disagreement over whether loneliness is a close correlate of depression or is entirely contained within the syndrome (Larsen et al., 1982; p. 219).

Young (1982) has demonstrated that some cases of loneliness respond to a therapy developed for depression although that is not the same as asserting the two conditions are related (p. 382). The fact that boredom and anxiety over facing oneself are also characteristics associated with depression keeps the loneliness-depression link from contradicting Mijuskovic's hypotheses.

The societal approach to loneliness operates on the premise that the incidence of loneliness has increased dramatically in recent years and postulates transformations of social structure as agents of the change. Gordon (1976) takes the broadest view:

> In the past, people either married and stayed married, or they never married and were spinsters and bachelors for a major portion of their adult lives. In either case they lived in social situations in which they were part of a definite community, linked together by family affiliation, work interest, place of residence, and common beliefs and rituals. Being part of a couple did not totally determine their status of a group (p. 195).
>
> In the past, engaging in the occupations and interests necessary for physical and emotional survival, people met other people who would be important to them in their personal lives.

And the more human scale of social, neighborhood, and work institutions was conducive to the forging of interpersonal relationships.

Today many community groupings that provided peripheral relationships and the common ground necessary for the formation of new relationships have disappeared. And finding people with whom to relate, far from being an outgrowth of social and work activity, becomes a major occupation in and of itself. As soon as a man or woman leaves college or high school that persons enters an unstructured world where most of the living and working conditions encountered foster not stable contact but anonymity and transiency. In such an environment the only possibility of a stable relationship remaining to many people is with one other person. If a couple relationship does not materialize. . . . the means for developing a stable social network are more limited and less apparent (pp. 196-197).

Gordon goes on to add that the situation for individuals is compounded by our tendency to view people who cannot find mates as deficient—as failures (pp. 197-198).

A further aggravation is what Gordon refers to as the loneliness business. Since many of the natural opportunities for singles to meet have disappeared, enterprises have arisen to serve this purpose—singles bars, singles cruises, and singles apartment complexes—or to profit from the unhappiness of the isolates—gurus, encounter groups, est, etc. Since none of these enterprises has a long-term interest in reducing the incidence of loneliness in our culture, Gordon feels they are motivated not to solve the problem, but to cash in on it (p. 198).

Flanders (1982) adds two entries to the list of social changes influencing the incidence of isolation. First, he notes we no longer observe a day of rest each week for people to spend with their families and friends (p. 175). We are much too busy doing our own thing. Even when we do it with other family members (as in shopping), the time actually spent in social interaction is considerably less than it would be at a meal or at a relaxed get-together.

Flanders' second observation is that most of the rest of the week is spent televiewing. In fact, televiewing uses up more of our lifetimes than any other activity save sleep. If a work year is defined as two thousand hours (forty hours per week × fifty weeks per year), then the average member of our society spends fifty-seven work years televiewing in his lifetime. Flanders' concern is that deciding to spend fifty-seven work years televiewing is also to decide not to spend fifty-seven work years participating in relationships (pp. 175-177). Of course, people do watch television with each other. However, during such occasions there is far less eye contact and other verbal and nonverbal interaction than there would be in a similar period of conversation. The quality is just not there (p. 156).

It should be noted that neither Flanders nor Gordon refer to how people felt in the past to make their cases. Whether people experienced different amounts of loneliness in previous times is incidental to their depictions of our current behavior.

However, individual choices about livelihoods and lifestyles were much narrower in the past than they are now. Under those conditions, I suspect people thought of themselves and each other in terms of their occupational and social roles (because they were so much more clearly defined). While this may have occasioned different identity conflicts from those we have today, it does not provide a basis for assuming anything about how comfortable individuals were with themselves in those circumstances.

Roles are really expectation sets directed at the role holders. As such, they provide no more realistic a basis for one's identity than do today's designer clothes. They do, however, make it very difficult for people to relate to one another as individuals. Relationships tend to be among roles and tend to be defined by expectation sets.

An interesting conjecture is whether our move away from a role-defined social structure was necessitated by the development of a complex economy, or whether it was a voluntary choice (a rejection of the constraints of roles) not possible before our economy became complex enough to support it.

In any event, without reference to the past, Gordon presents a convincing case that many unmarried adults currently spend a great deal of their lives in a frustrating quest for a fulfilling union. And while one may wish for some quantitative data on how we do spend our Sundays, Flanders' assertion that the average person spends 57 work years watching television is a simple statistical fact.

The problem is that the cases apparently contradict each other. When combined they seem to say that we find solitary existence so uncomfortable that we are driven to marriage. Yet, whatever relational rewards marriage offers, they are not enough to prevent us from spending 57 work years in the passive isolation of televiewing.

Flanders hypothesizes that maintaining relationships requires a great investment of time and effort, and that we find it easier to choose an instant gratification like watching television (p. 156). Such reasoning simply masks the original contradiction, as it presumes that a natural drive toward rewarding relationships is being perverted.

Several simpler hypotheses suggest themselves. The drive toward sharing may not be as strong as is commonly felt. People may be seeking pair relationships because that is the model their experience forces them toward (that is, the role society expects). Or it may be that the satisfactions which relationships provide require fewer interactions than most investigators assume.

It is interesting to note that Mijuskovic's conjectures fit the situation well. His ranking of a drive to alleviate loneliness immediately after those for food and shelter explain the priorities. The social expectations of paired living could account for the initial emphasis on seeking a union. However, having a partner does not cure our fear of facing ourselves, so we hide from ourselves in front of the television.

It could also be that the presence of an accepting companion makes a qualitative difference and is therefore sought as a precondition for living a natural lifestyle of limited interaction.

Whatever one's interpretation of loneliness, one is stuck with the fact that a large number of people spend a great deal of their time with a lot less interaction than most approaches to loneliness presume. For education, the central question is in which direction it ought to lead: toward an acceptance of our fundamental isolation (which would make to relate or not to relate a value-free choice), or toward the rewards of deep and meaningful relationships, which presumes that the question of our fundamental isolation or aloneness may be of minor importance?

Is Religion the Answer?

One would expect that religion would have much to say about so profound a human problem as loneliness. In fact, the major Christian denominations seem to ignore the problem. A recent review of the publications in the Yale Divinity School Library revealed only a handful of references to the topic. Most of these address it explicitly as a

minor concern, in stark contrast to (and in total ignorance
of) the secular literature on the subject.

For one trained in an academic approach to research, a
brief exposure to religious publications is distressing. Most
of the articles, when analyzed, were rendered meaningless
by either incomprehensible sentence structure, incoherent
reasoning, or a combination of the two. A representative
example is Sebastian Moore's *The Inner Loneliness* (1982),
which begins with

> The inner loneliness arises out of a paradox; that that in us
> which impells us to form relationships is, it seems, destined to
> be forever lonely. For that which impells me to form relation-
> ships and to embark on every other creative enterprise is the
> sense of myself as special, unique, and without price; but no
> one can know me as I thus know myself, no one can touch me
> as I thus feel myself, no one can be present to me as I am thus
> present to myself. So there is a loneliness in each person that
> no other person can relieve (p. 1).

Moore then goes on (pp. 7-14) to categorize so many
attributes of the human psyche that one is bewildered with
the distinctions, and their assumed interrelationships: reflexive self-awareness and non-reflexive self-awareness,
self-love, three states of desire "to want to be with another," *ad nauseam* for the entire book.

The few religious publications that were comprehensible
were flawed by their ignorance of the empirical secular
writing on the topic.

Empirical concerns seemed absent. For example, Jeffrey
Soboson (1978) speculates that nontransient loneliness is
uncommon because the condition would be so psychologically painful that it would produce either a psychosis or
suicidal depression (p. 105). He postulates that humanity is

protected from these dire fates because "in each of us there is a 'force' that of its own accord propels us away from too much and too long a loneliness. We become involved, seemingly despite ourselves, in the world around us (p. 196).

It is difficult to come to terms with Moore, Soboson, et al. One explanation is offered by Robinson (1980). Writing on loneliness, he offers reflexive defenses of gibberish by noting that Christ spoke in parables and by offering this quotation from Kierkegaard: "Religious understanding must rest on a relinquishment of the complacent belief that objectivity guarantees truth" (pp. 196-199).

Poor scholarship and lack of an empirical approach seems a much better hypothesis. Reasoning which is wholly inferential seems appropriate for theological topics which do not lend themselves to hypothesis testing. Even though centuries have passed since the trial of Galileo, many in the religious community seem still to widely accept this mode of reasoning for nontheological areas.

It is easy to speculate that the discipline which must be needed to keep inferential theological reasoning within bounds narrow enough to give it utility is not widely understood by the religious community. Poor scholars grasp only the mystery of inductive theology. When they are confronted with other subjects which they do not understand, they try to elicit meaning by writing mysteriously. Some, like Moore, give names to their thought fragments, as if invoking magic to make the fragments both real and explanatory.

Less easy to explain is the silence of the literature with regard to loneliness. Much of the lack of recognition of loneliness among religious thinkers might be due, in part, to religion's inherent conservatism and its slowness to respond to social changes.

Religion has traditionally underpinned the values of society. Until recently, society has been structured to provide its members with roles, and religion has functioned to support this ordering. The lack of recognition of loneliness as an important issue may be a reflection of religion's failure to recognize that society is moving away from roles and the identities they impose upon individuals. The religious educator must be keenly aware of this.

Another factor may be that the denial of the importance of roles is threatening to members of the religious community who often define their own identities as perceptions of idealized religious roles. Some evidence exists for this conjecture. Houck and Dawson (1978) report that the typical "seminarian is less inclined to self-evaluation and self-judgment than expected and does not appear to compare himself unflavorably with others" (p. 1136).

Religious educators may have a problem with the religious connotations of "loneliness." A natural and fundamental concern of religion is a person's relationship with God. There is a long tradition of regarding loneliness as a symptom of an individual's estrangement from God. This estrangement or loneliness is felt to indicate a lack or loss of faith. Because faith is an expression of a person's free will, overcoming this estrangement is frequently felt to be a task that must be accomplished by the individual.

For example, the only nontransient loneliness Soboson (1978) recognizes is an isolation from God. He believes this commonly occurs in three circumstances: 1) an individual like Camus [his reference] "feels isolated from God because God seems continually to ignore or misapprehend the question of human suffering; 2) an individual's prayers are unanswered; or 3) a member of the clergy [for reasons not given] loses his or her faith" (p. 107).

Soboson has no advice to offer those afflicted with these lonelinesses. His concluding two sentences indicate he feels they suffer in traps of their own perceptions: "Experiences of acceptance by God, in short, may easily get lost among experiences of his presumed unacceptance. It is, without trying to speak too boldly, largely a matter of emphasis of how the individual interprets for his faith the events which try his existence" (p. 108).

In a more encouraging vein, McCann (1977-78) reported on a counseling service in Pennsylvania that assisted over three thousand convent members who were having difficulties coming to terms with some of the Vatican II reforms. Prior to Vatican II, most convent members lived a life of communal isolation (Lieblich, 1983, pp. 12-21). Communication and other interactions were kept to an absolute minimum. Instead of relating to each other, each member of the convent focused on her own life with God (McCann, p. 62).

The reforms initiated by Vatican II required members of religious communities to communicate and develop relationships with one another and to make a wider range of choices about their personal lives.

McCann reported that "for persons whose lives have been dedicated to a denial of self, the acceptance of that self's basic human needs is painful and confusing." She noted that before the nuns could cope with communication and interrelationships, they first had to deal with the anxiety of establishing their own identities. Prior to Vatican II's reforms, they had an "unambiguous, idealized self." Now, they had to decide what they "should look like, be, and do" (pp. 62-63).

The parallels between these nuns deprived of aspects of their role-derived identities and laity who also can no longer establish their identities in terms of roles and role expectations are striking. Although McCann did not indicate she was aware of the problem in the lay population, her observations and insights could be readily transferred, though the correspondence between the two situations is not complete. The nuns had an advantage not generally applicable to the lay population since they had the support of the other members of their communities who were all experiencing much the same difficulties at the same time.

Religion must address this problem sensibly, and external pressure for change is very much evident. As Gordon (1976) notes, the marketplace is already producing a plethora of alternatives: gurus, encounter groups, est, etc. (pp. 247-307). To survive this competition, orthodox religion must either become more like it or provide a better service.

With so little understanding of the phenomenon, it is difficult to choose an appropriate direction for current religious education.

A very large portion of the population has difficulties in relating to people as individuals, due to a lack of sufficient self-awareness to establish their own identities, yet Young (1982) found that merely getting people to overcome their fears of being alone often removed a whole set of syndromes that had prevented them from establishing viable social relationships.

Too little is understood about the nature of human happiness (or self-fulfillment) to take any steps toward engineering people to fit a particular view of good social adjustment which is an oft-suggested "remedy" for loneliness.

All previous societies were organized on the basis of roles and role-expectations out of economic necessity. The fact that these roles and their expectations were abandoned as soon as economic conditions permitted casts doubt on most generalizations about what "natural human behavior" is (e.g., that man is obviously a social animal).

An individual who is taught to be self-aware and intro- spective can make his own choices about relationships. One who has been comfortably integrated into someone else's definition of an appropriate number of relationships with appropriate degrees of intimacy has lost his individuality. The religious educator must balance *both* aspects of this problem.

So much of what passes for insight in religious education and pastoral counseling is really little more than unfound- ed assumptions about the nature of reality. There certainly is room in the human experience for mystery and "unknowables," but a review of current religious literature suggests that there is also room for considerably more empirical exploration.

Loneliness is certainly both ubiquitous and inescapable, at least occasionally. This, however, does not exempt the religious educator or counselor from addressing the prob- lem with the same rigor that one would expect from any other honest academician.

In attempting to be of help, the religious educator must first *define* the event he/she seeks to explore clearly—and in behaviorally anchored terms. That is, the definition of loneliness they accept should have a clear set of observable behaviors associated with them; we should be able to see from how the person acts what might be the interior expe- rience. With loneliness, one would observe the person's affect as well as social skills, community involvement, and *conscious* sense of being isolated. There would also be evi- dent actions and feelings which the person would emit which would suggest that he or she was "unlovable."

After a definition has been accepted (and there are many workable ones in the social science literature), it is necessary for the religious educator and counselor to distinguish the specific conditions of loneliness. Is it *chronic, situational,* or *transient?*

1) *Chronic loneliness* will be evident from a person's long-term inability and deficit in relating to others. It will often be characterized by an impoverished social system which has endured for years.

2) *Situational loneliness* arises from an individual's *present* set of circumstances. It results from a disruption of the person's social interrelationships. Examples of this are relocation, death of a spouse.

3) *Transient loneliness* arises from occasional feelings of isolation and these are universally experienced by most sensitive and psychologically minded individuals.

The designation of the type of loneliness is critical for the proposed suggestion of an appropriate intervention. If an individual has been chronically lonely, this will say much to the educator about the etiology and intervention techniques which are useful. Chronically lonely people usually benefit from desensitization of social anxieties and from social skills training.

Desensitization of social anxiety is a useful psychological tool for any educator, but the religious educator has a distinct advantage of having available a believing, supportive community of faith—people who can use their communal/group cohesiveness for supporting individuals and offering them positive regard.

The religious educator may also call upon group activities and class work in helping individuals develop their social skills abilities whether these include a sense of drama (acting out a biblical story, dancing/singing a psalm, being on a parish board, etc.) or participation in liturgy. All this may—and should—be undertaken within a supportive communal environment. The potent capacity which group membership holds for protecting and educating as well as confronting individuals is a natural resource for the educator in religion. It is the most powerful tool available and one which should form the basis for most interventions with lonely individuals.

This communal/group experience offers even the chronically lonely individual a chance at what Yalom refers to as a "corrective recapitulation" of the primary family group where many of the seeds of isolation were sown (see the chapter on infancy and childhood). The powerful assistance group interaction offers include, according to Yalom:

1. *Imparting of information.* This enables individuals to explore the reality that all peoples experience loneliness in some ways throughout the life cycle. Such a book as this one can be used as a study aid and stimulus material to trigger group discussion and interaction.

2. *Installation of hope.* While all groups install hope (or can), the faith community is predicated on a hope as its foundation. Hence it is considerably easier for the leader/educator to reference faith points of hope, refer to other group member's experience, and/or call on commonly held religious beliefs.

3. *Universality.* This characteristic of group process confirms the fact that certain experiences are common to all people. Universality affords individuals an opportunity to generalize from their own experiences and to explore the commonality of their experiences with others.

4. *Altruism.* This is a sense of giving and sharing with others. This characteristic of group offers individuals a chance to see how others give and take and also affords an opportunity to challenge and develop the social skills so critical in alleviating loneliness.

5. *Corrective recapitulation of the family group.* This aspect of group offers a lonely person an opportunity to experience once again the basic issues of trust/ mistrust as well as acceptance, affirmation, and accountability. Particularly relevant for the religious educator is the opportunity of enabling individuals to become bonded with their faith community within a context of free choice and affirmation. It is critical here that the religious/ethical educator deftly intertwine accountability and incorporation in a manner which enhances the individual.

6. *Development of socialization techniques.* This characteristic of group enables an individual to *practice* social skills. This, according to current research, is the most critical area in learning deficit for lonely people. It appears to be a vicious circle which involves individuals who feel rejected and unloved while, at the same time they continue to act in ways which are clearly deficient in people-attracting behaviors. Within a group, individuals are enabled to correct their deficient skills and to learn new ones through discussion with others and by observing modeling behaviors of the religious/ethical educator and group leaders.

7. *Imitative Behavior.* This aspect of group enables an individual an opportunity to see other people in *action* and to help correct deficit learning and behaviors. This flows directly from the socialization functions of groups.

8. *Interpersonal behavior.* This enables one to evaluate and get feedback on how they impact on other people. Nowhere else is the opportunity so abundant. The group/faith community is a natural human behavior laboratory wherein an individual can learn

and apply. The religious/ethical educator has an opportunity to enable individuals to explore a repertoire of behavior as well as to apply these behaviors. The empirically minded educator has a built-in opportunity to engage in the best of learning situations with clear "before" and "after" measures available.

9. *Group Cohesiveness.* This aspect of group enables the lonely individual to benefit from their growing skills as they also experience themselves as part of a larger whole. It is here—and only within this context— that the religious/ethical educator can enable one to expand his or her skills and to learn to moderate less appealing personality styles for the sake of the larger whole. The entire community of faith, as understood in contemporary terms, demands that notions of alienation, narcissism, sin, etc., are intelligible only in terms of community integration, cooperation, and lovability.

10. *Catharsis.* This is the ability to "purge" oneself of feelings. Clearly, the group/community enables one to "check out" his or her feelings as well as to cleanse them. Obviously, over many years, individuals who have been rejected and lonely and who sustain this indirectly by deficient social skills have an opportunity to purge these emotions within the context of an integrated and cohesive group. They are empowered to understand, empathically, the behaviors of others in the group who have similar problems and to use the group creatively as an opportunity to correct and "clean out" their own sense of failure, unlovability, etc.

As can be seen, the group experience conducted by the religious/ethical educator is a powerful tool for intervening in the chronic and situational aspects of loneliness. Situational loneliness, unlike chronic loneliness, responds to reassurance, which is an indirect and potent aspect of group membership.

When I speak of group process above, I am not suggesting that all religious educators be group psychotherapists but, rather, that they be familiar with and competent in handling the ordinary process of group living, whether it be in doing committee work with individuals or the more personally oriented growth groups.

Some Other Concerns

The lonely individual is often obvious to the sensitive religious educator in a number of ways. Often they come to us self-labeled; however the teacher must be prepared to *infer* this based on the individual's *behaviors*. Before the educator approaches an individual, it is necessary that the person give behavioral *evidence* of dissatisfaction. This is most often evident in the individual's self-evaluation which on first blush appears similar to depression—and may be exactly that. The "giveaway" is often that the person's loneliness and depression in the case of the chronically lonely is universally characterized by a clear social deficit.

But how is this deficit determined and what does it look like? Social deficit has many definitions which vary according to the theoretical position. However, all definitions agree on the following:

1. In the socially deficient person, the basic need for intimacy is being inadequately discharged.
2. There is a lack of an intimate partner or community.
3. There is a felt lack of status such as marriage.

These characteristics above all have in common one absence—*contact*. But what *kinds* of contact actually enable the religious/ethical educator to alleviate loneliness?

1. An emphasis on *social events* has been helpful. That is to say, an approach which emphasizes the benefits and rewards of society such as conversation, theater, church, encourage an individual to increase the frequency of these positive experiences. The high frequency of positive social activity helps compensate for the lack of an intimate partner—in part at least.

2. An emphasis on *social relationships* helps persons develop particular types of relationships—love, friendships, and confidant relationships. It is critical here that the religious educator point out that *no* single relationship can provide individuals with all they desire. The current spate of advertisements and popularized psychology which promise immediate and universal gratification are clearly inappropriate. All individuals need and can have figures of both attachment and friendship/social activity. It is critical that the religious educator focus on the social network. Since the community/group of faith offers an immediate group experience, the educator can speak from firsthand experience. *Never* promise an individual that intimacy with a special someone will be attained. This is simply not something anyone can guarantee. Often one finds that individuals who have moderated their social deficit and increased their social skills will expand that ability into the arena of interpersonal intimacy, but there is *no* causal link and no reputable educator will suggest it exists.

At the same time one is encouraging social activities, it can be useful to help individuals explore social *solitary* activities. This has two distinct advantages and involves enabling individuals to overcome their fear of isolation by finding some positive aspects of "doing their own thing." A developing ability to be occupied with one's own interests and to get rewards from them increases individuals' sense of personal power and control over their lives—a precondition of relinquishing feelings of self-negativity.

The religious/ethical educator must tread a difficult road here. While utilizing group/communal interaction as a powerful tool, the educator must balance a sense of the solitary self and creative rewards flowing from that with growing social skills and rewards. The theoretical progress of this skills training might look like the following:

1. Begin with having individuals engage in personal solitary activities.
2. This should then move into group interaction.
3. This should develop into some potential friendships.
4. *Possibly,* this might move to intimacy with someone special.

For educational purposes, the structure for alleviating individual loneliness appears to begin with an individual emphasis which then moves to a group-based interaction with the final goal of a one-on-one interpersonal activity with a hope for special intimacy. This special intimacy can never be guaranteed, but for those with theistic beliefs one can call on the specialness of individual lives and creation as well as relationship with a loving creator.

All the above intervention techniques involve a hierarchy of activities which demand careful and individualized preparation by the educator. These include a hierarchal development of skills from least threatening to most challenging.

A normal sequence of training which the religious/ethical educator might undertake would involve simple exercises with these individuals which include:

1. *Initiating conversation and discussion.* Within the context of the parish group/classroom the religious/ethical educator might encourage individuals to begin conversations.

2. *Giving and accepting compliments.* This would involve the student in actually accepting responsibility for a job/service well done. Again, based on modeling of the educator, the student has an opportunity to confirm others and receive their support as well.

3. *Developing tolerance for periods of silence.* There the religious/ethical educator has the lead. Silence is often the condition of meditation and reflection, and individuals with religious beliefs can often deflect their uneasiness by turning their minds to prayer—even if only momentarily. This growth in handling silence enables individuals to "try out" their new skills in a group *without* necessarily feeling that they are at fault. They will also have the opportunity of observing how uncomfortable with silence many other people are— and how they handle it.

4. *Increasing physical attractiveness and appearance.* This is an often forgotten dimension in education. While I am not arguing in favor of rigid codes of dress, it *is* important to aid one in being groomed well and dressed appropriately. Interestingly, many of the people I interviewed who expressed high levels of loneliness had a recurrent problem regarding self-presentation. In addition to poor social skills, many also display poor self-care. I am not suggesting that "beauty" is the secret, but, in view of recent social science research, it is significant that one's presentation of self clearly reflects an inner sense of value. Behavioral research increasingly suggests that external activities often increase one's repertoire of behaviors and become internalized as positive self-regard.

5. *Becoming more adept at nonverbal communication.* Many individuals are unaware that their nonverbal behaviors clearly suggest they don't "want" people near them. The social skills deficit is clearly reflected in a

nonverbal negative attitude toward others who *might* form the basis of social activities and/or possible friendships.

6. *Awareness and growth in appropriate self-revelation.* It is critical that individuals learn how and *what* to reveal to others. Many lonely people report either over-caution or inappropriately intimate self-disclosure which results in distancing others rather than attracting them. Here the educator in religion and ethics has a unique opportunity in exploring levels of intimacy and correlating them with levels of incorporation within the community. The revelation one gives of self to a new parish/class member is quite different from what one uses with a long-term, valued friend. Within the parish community, many options are available.

Prevention

It should be clear that loneliness remains an integral part of the human experience yet there are still things which individuals might do to ameliorate and/or prevent chronic loneliness. The religious educator can call here on the tradition of aloneness in Christianity as well as other faiths and may use these to challenge the current social myths effectively.

Certainly, we need to challenge the current cultural myth that there is something suspect to being alone. This is clearly reflected in the media hype and commercials where the goal of all of living seems to be finding that "one" relationship.

We also need to grow in toleration and acceptance of various lifestyles. The churches are a major impediment since they often seem more concerned about upholding doctrine than concern for the lived experience of people.

Friendship can provide great support even for one without that "someone special."

We need to explore our architecture as well. It is clear from organizational research that individuals react variously to different environments. Some arrangements of furniture, etc., alienate and separate people, others encourage interaction. This becomes evident when one simply thinks of an employer who keeps his/her door open to employees as opposed to the executive locked away behind the mahogany door.

Self-help is the greatest preventive. Individuals who have worked through aspects of their loneliness and who have achieved some improvement have a moral imperative to help others. This can be utilized much as Alcoholics Anonymous is used.

The religious educator needs to contour his/her intervention to the developmental needs of the person he/she is working with. What is helpful for the adolescent may not be useful for the aged person. Their experiences arise from radically different cultural bases and these differences need to be honored.

As always, there is a need for continued and rigorous research into the interface of religion, psychology, and education. One cannot be used without the other—at least not for those who take social science and human growth seriously.

Finally, this book must fail since the human experience transcends our capacity to analyze it definitely. We remain with a partial mystery for the human experience as one of *both* companionship and aloneness. However, it appears that the vicissitudes of living and the rhythm of the life cycle often focus on the awareness of our aloneness more acutely.

What remains particularly human is the way in which we

deal with our aloneness. We can use it as a form of withdrawal and then it becomes loneliness, or we can use it as an incentive to move toward others and God; then it becomes solitude. What we cannot do is ignore it or simply placate it. Aloneness is for so many people too close to death to find ignoring or placating satisfying.

Our pastoral and educational experience indicates that aloneness is a crucial area of maturation. What do we expect finally of family and community, work, prayer, commitment, vows? These cannot eliminate loneliness or aloneness. They can, however, give us strategies for addressing the creative possibilities of finding others and God in our own restrictions.

There remains, after all we have suggested and researched, an asceticism of confronting human aloneness within the limitations and opportunities provided at different times during the life cycle. There is also a skill, mystery, and maturation which increases as we creatively engage with loneliness. Loneliness is not being alone, and as we become able to balance a sense of solitude and aloneness with loneliness we gain greater deftness in living. Loneliness is death-bringing; solitude can be life-bringing. Loneliness which goes unchallenged results in being conquered by our restrictions, while aloneness enables us to transcend some limitation and become related to the mystery of life, other people, and God.

We must always contrast the paradigms of aloneness in modern life—and this remains a unique capacity of the religious/ethical educator. Aloneness in modern life is viewed differently than in the religious tradition. Our shared history as Christians and our involvement in the present are both lived in awareness of profound aloneness. Human decisions, affective moments can be shared, it is true, but they must first be claimed and possessed. Thus silence, reflection, reverence, examination can become celebrations of how we join our aloneness to the greater experience of being part of humanity and a faith community.

Some of the greatest religious thinkers have concerned themselves with this approach to loneliness and aloneness. Fot example, St. Ignatius uses aloneness as a departure point for discernment in the *Spiritual Exercises:* silence, prayer, and reflection require aloneness but are preconditions to being "with God"; they become desolation when they become distant or "hidden from God."

Although we continue to research and explore, our task remains to analyze the rhythms and vicissitudes of the human life cycle and to examine the kinds of loneliness which contour the human experience as well as the creative and developmentally appropriate strategies for addressing it.

References

Cutrona, C. E. Transition to college: Loneliness and the process of social adjustment. In L. A. Peplau & D. Perlman (Eds.), *Loneliness: A sourcebook of current theory, research, and therapy.* New York: John Wiley & Sons, 1982.

Ellison, C. W. Loneliness: A social development analysis. *Journal of Psychology and Theology,* Winter 1978, 6, 3-17.

Fischer, C. S. & Phillips, S. L. Who is alone? Social characteristics of people in small networks. In L. A. Peplau & D. Perlman (Eds.), *Loneliness: A sourcebook of current theory, research, and therapy.* New York: John Wiley & Sons, 1982.

Flanders, J. P. A general systems approach to loneliness. In L. A. Peplau & D. Perlman (Eds.), *Loneliness: A sourcebook of current theory, research, and therapy.* New York: John Wiley & Sons, 1982.

Gordon, S. *Lonely in America.* New York: Simon & Schuster, 1976.

Houck, R. L. & Dawson, J. G. Comparative study of persisters and leavers in seminary training. *Psychological Reports,* 1978, 42, 1131-1137.

Larsen, R. Csikszenimihalyi, M. & Graef, R. Time alone in daily experience: Loneliness or renewal. In L. A. Peplau & D. Perlman (Eds.), *Loneliness: A sourcebook of current theory, research, and therapy.* New York: John Wiley & Sons, 1982.

Lieblich, J. The cloistered life. *New York Times Magazine*, 10 July 1983, pp. 12-21.

McCann, M. The best—the worst of times (a reflection on stress as it affects religious women). *Journal of Pastoral Counseling*, Fall-Winter 1977-1978, 12, 61-64.

Mijuskovic, B. Loneliness: An interdisciplinary approach. *Psychiatry*, May 1977, 40, 113-132.

Moor, S. *The inner loneliness*. New York: Crossroad, 1982.

Peplau, L. A., Miceli, M. & Morasch, B. Loneliness and self-evaluation. In L. A. Peplau & D. Perlman (Eds.), *Loneliness: A sourcebook of current theory, research, and therapy*. New York: John Wiley & Sons, 1982.

Peplau, L. A. & Perlman, D. *Loneliness: A sourcebook of current theory, research, and therapy*. New York: John Wiley & Sons, 1982.

Robinson, E. Loneliness and communication. *Theology*, May 1980, 83, 195-203.

Rogers, C. *Carl Rogers on encounter groups*. New York: Harper & Row, 1970.

Russell, D. The measurement of loneliness. In L. A. Peplau & D. Perlman (Eds.), *Loneliness: A sourcebook of current theory, research, and therapy*. New York: John Wiley & Sons, 1982.

Soboson, J. G. Loneliness and faith. *Journal of Psychology and Theology*, Spring 1978, 61, 104-109.

Weiss, R. S. Issues in the study of loneliness. In L. A. Peplau & D. Perlman (Eds.), Loneliness: A sourcebook of current theory, research, and therapy. New York: John Wiley & Sons, 1982.

Young, J. E. Loneliness, depression, and cognitive therapy: Theory and application. In L. A. Peplau & D. Perlman (Eds.), *Loneliness: A sourcebook of current theory, research, and therapy*. New York: John Wiley & Sons, 1982.

Index